The Squirrel Trap

C. A. LIEN

The Squirrel Trap
By Clark Lien

Cover photo of Mt. St. Helens circa. 1980, reportedly the last photo taken by the now deceased, Richard Lasher.

Copyright July 2022
Published July 2024

ISBN 979-8-35096-818-7

Table of Contents

Preface

While their presence and harmless appearance may suggest innocence, squirrels retain a destructive nature and can cause various health risks to humans. Squirrels tend to be comfortable in the open but can make a quick exit when trouble nears. Similar traits can often be found in modern society's politicians. The comparison is seldom made, but as I'll demonstrate, it is a useful one and an image I often applied in overcoming the frustrations provided to me during my government career.

Squirrels are amazing thieves; when attempting to catch them, you must select bait that is difficult to steal. Solid bait should be larger than the mesh openings of the trap; unshelled peanuts work well. Strawberries also work as bait, although in the case of a politician, cash is a good substitute. It is said that squirrels lose 80 percent of the nuts they hide, which seems proportional to the amount of taxes wasted by politicians.

It is inhumane to leave an animal trapped for an extended period, therefore traps must be checked frequently so that the squirrel does not become hungry, thirsty, or anxious. An agitated squirrel, like an angry politician, is dangerous when it feels trapped and can cause an incredible amount of damage.

When releasing a squirrel, avoid direct contact by wearing gloves, and holding the trap by its handle. A squirrel bite may carry bacteria and can lead to injury. Upon release, squirrels should not be allowed back into your yard. Similarly, once a politician has shown a desire for your property or for the confiscation of your rights, it is best to distance yourself from their influence. This will help prevent financial injury and loss of freedom.

Reducing attractions, such as removing bird feeders, helps to prevent pesky squirrels from returning. Limit accessibility: trim tree branches and apply repellents. In the case of experienced, ego-driven politicians, complete avoidance is the best way to prevent financial injury.

CHAPTER 1

Childhood

The cold, hard steel pressing against the back of my head felt like a synopsis for my adult life. "Click" was the next sound I heard; the misfire stunned me. Despite my confused state, I realized that if it had discharged and I was still alive, I would have been left with the distinct taste of gunpowder residue. Instead of being relieved, I became agitated; my plan had succumbed to failure. This was my fifty-first birthday and the second time I survived a bullet intent on taking my life. The first had been twenty years earlier.

The previous year, for my fiftieth birthday, I was the proud recipient of front-row concert tickets—a gift from my girlfriend. I was set to see my favorite rock band in Las Vegas, Nevada. It was the perfect gift; ever since my first live concert, I have been addicted to the crowd's radiant energy. Unfortunately, the COVID-19 pandemic had a different agenda, causing the show to be cancelled. The beginning of what were supposed to be my golden years were quickly becoming wooden ones, providing complimentary splinters.

Thankfully, my childhood was not such a disappointing period in my life. I was raised in the small city of Gresham, located in the great state of Oregon. This was the ideal environment to grow up in for three young adventurous boys like my two brothers and me. I was the middle child, which often felt like riding in the middle of a single cab truck with two other occupants. I would ask my mother, "Why did you stick me in the middle?" Though she, of course, had no reasonable answer to my childish question. She is of German descent and has a stern but kind disposition. She stands only five feet tall with brown hair and brown eyes. My father was of Norwegian descent, a tall, slender man with sharp blue eyes and blond hair. I have many of my mother's traits, while my brothers' appearances are more like that of my father.

My parents met in Huntington Beach, California, where they were married, purchased a home and had two boys, my older brother and myself. Just before my second birthday, they moved to Oregon to start a new life. My younger brother was born a year after the move. I was against having another sibling, but at the age of only five I wasn't old enough to have a vote in that decision. My mother said he was planned, though I thought differently. By looking at him you could not tell, but I believed he was an accident. Though as it turned out, if he was an accident, he was a good one; he became my childhood scapegoat and, as an adult, my confidant.

The reason for my family's move to Oregon was the loss of my father's job as a machinist in California. My mother worked as an accountant, which made her job more mobile. With no support from their immediate family, they set out in search of stable employment in this new state. Oregon was an easy choice for my mother because her parents already resided here, and her career was more flexible. Despite our new proximity to my grandparents, we didn't visit them much, unless it was for a holiday or one of my father's hunting trips. I believe this was in part due to my parents' attempts at protecting us from exposure to my grandparents' codependent relationship with alcohol. The area offered cruel winters and many here turned to the vice of alcohol to help ease the effect of the cold.

Oregon could be at times a harsh place to live, but my parents loved being surrounded by nature. The constant rain and occasional snowstorms were what made this place so green and beautiful. For a young boy, snow was the best part of growing up here. In winter, building snow forts and having snowball fights became a part of my daily routine. I highly recommend a good snowball fight to get your blood pumping. A huge grin could always be found on any kid's face as they launched a perfectly made snowball at their opponent. This was particularly true if the snowball's target was their sibling.

My older brother's snowballs educated me on the benefits of staying out of harm's way. I may have constructed the best forts, but my brother made the hardest snowballs. His snowball constructing talents helped me discover that I was better off in a well-constructed fort. This motivated me to make quality snow forts. While he made his snowballs, I would claim the highest ground to build my fort. My snow fort would keep me warm and out of his line of fire until he ran out of ammunition.

The trick to winning a snowball fight, like any fight, was not the ammunition but the quality of your protection. However, this perspective on life; choosing to pursue security over risk, may not have served me well as an adult. I would come to understand that taking risks was a part of life and the only way to truly prosper. I fear that the regret of not experiencing more of life by taking chances may plague many people.

TRAVEL

Oregon winter storms may have supplied a source of entertainment for a young boy, but they were not as enjoyable for adults. I had many rainy days off from school, running and jumping into mud puddles. But for my father, having a safe commute to work meant scraping the ice from the windshield of his old truck, then driving several treacherous roads to reach his place of employment.

My father was a proud blue-collar worker. After arriving in Oregon, he started work as a lumberjack before procuring a position in his previous trade as a machinist. He made parts for heavy mining equipment, and his clothes all smelled of fresh-cut steel. He often found enjoyment in explaining the difference between a blue-collar worker and a white-collar worker. He would say, "A white-collar worker is the one with the garage full of tools who lacks the ability to use them, and the blue-collar worker is the one who knows how to operate these tools but lacks the means to access them." He would conclude his statement by saying, "The right tools in the wrong hands will lead to a less-than-desired outcome." Maybe in these statements he was just trying to express his disdain toward his supervisors, though I never asked, so I guess I'll never know.

Even with his difficult occupation, he somehow always strived to maintain a kind disposition with his boys. He enjoyed surprising us and in his lunch box, he would bring home a daily treat for us. This is something he learned from his mother; the joy of a tasty treat when he came home from school. The snack was usually some type of candy he had bought from the vending machine at work. I am sure he did this to see the smiles on our faces when we ran to retrieve what he had brought for us.

His three sons meant the world to my father. Whenever possible he would share with us nature's wonders, we went fishing and hunting regularly. He took us as far as his income would allow, from the Sea Lion Caves and Redwood Forest on the coast, to the Multnomah Falls on the Columbia River. The Multnomah Falls recreational area was a short drive from our home in Gresham. The first time my father took me to the falls, with my boyish energy, all I could think about was climbing to the top. Witnessing the cascading water falling from this massive cliff was truly inspiring. Although I never made it to the top, just being in its presence made me respect the water's incredible power.

California's Redwood Forest was also a wakening experience for me. Life can adopt a new meaning that will latch onto your soul, when watching eagles soar overhead, while lying under a redwood tree that rises three hundred feet into the air. My father sharing trips to places like this provided me with a meaning to the word respect. These are places I will certainly never forget and memories that have stayed with me, guiding me through the difficult times in my life.

My father understood that these places had to be seen to be experienced. He knew that life's lessons were best learned outside of a classroom. I was very thankful that he took the time to show us these natural wonders. Seeing them helped me to realize that they were not just meant to be appreciated for their physical beauty, but they were also there to inspire and humble us. I now believe boys specifically need to see and feel nature to help us calm our zealous frustrations and find inner peace.

DRIVING

Most local destinations in Oregon were accessed by vehicle but travel here required caution as the weather determined the road conditions. Car accidents were common on Oregon's rain-slicked roads, and my father was no stranger to this phenomenon. Though most were not his fault, he was involved in many car accidents where vehicles met their demise. His demeanor changed while behind the wheel of a car; to him there was no justification for bad driving. For most people cars were a form of transportation, but for him they were a tool used to teach other drivers proper road etiquette.

A large cloth bag full of small rocks sat just behind my father's driver's seat. I would often witness him reaching behind his seat into this old cloth bag to procure one of these rocks. When he encountered what he considered to be a bad driver, he would throw the rock out of the driver's side window toward the other vehicle. I would cringe when the rock left his hand, waiting to hear the ting sound as it bounced off the side of a passing car. His intention of getting the other driver's attention often worked, although the lesson he was trying to teach was seldom ever successfully achieved.

My mother's usual response to my father's inappropriate actions was to exclaim, "Sugar gets more than salt!" This of course meant that he would receive a better reaction from people if he was nicer to them. In reply he had his own prepared cynical response to being questioned about the occurrence of an incident while driving. He explained how, according to him, an irresponsible driver making the crucial error of conducting an illegal vehicle maneuver in front of him would cause him temporary amnesia as to the location of his vehicle's brakes. This was his eloquent way of explaining why he would purposely hit a car that cut him off.

Riding in a car with my father taught me the importance of wearing my seat belt. My mother also furnished me with wisdom regarding driving, which was to always yield the right of way when at a four-way intersection. I was thankful for these lessons, particularly my mother's. Letting other cars go first has served me well; it's a cheap easy way to buy a person's approval and gain their sympathy, as people tend to remember kind gestures.

Only once was I with my father during his spree of automobile accidents. He was behind the wheel of his orange-colored, single-cab, 1970 Chevy pickup truck, when the driver of a shiny, new red Corvette made an illegal left turn in front of him. This was the biggest mistake the driver of the Corvette would make that day. Just before the collision, my father reached over the middle of the truck's bench seat, and with his right hand grasped my seat belt cinching it tight. He then proceeded forward through the intersection deliberately striking the Corvette on its driver's side. The impact occurred at approximately forty miles per hour and was jarring to say the least. Thankfully, because of my father, I was securely fastened in my seat and barely moved.

After the truck came to a stop, my father looked over to see that I was not hurt. He then went to check on the other driver and found that the driver of the corvette somehow survived the accident with only minor injuries. Though the same could not be said of his car. The life of the Corvette's driver was spared, but his car was not. The force of the hit from my father's solid steel truck shattered the front end of the Corvette. This is how I found out that Corvettes were made of fiberglass. It's amazing how much physical damage can be caused by unrestrained power.

CAR

Without knowing my father and hearing the stories of his accidents, most people thought he was just unlucky. Little did they know of the truth about his unforgiving attitude toward other drivers. The minimum driving age in Oregon was fifteen—scary for parents but exciting for young adults. Driver's licenses here were so easy to get that kids used to say they could be found in a Cracker Jack box. This also happens to be a question my father would often ask other drivers, if this is where they procured their license. Unfortunately for my brother, there was no license in his box of candied popcorn; he was forced to take a test for his.

My older brother was excited when it came time to get his first driver's license. I didn't understand his feeling until I had the opportunity to get my own. Having a license was different in the 1980s, the expense was much less, and it was more about gaining freedom. Public transportation at the time was worse, and accessing stores was not as convenient. A car was the chance to explore beyond the reach of your bicycle.

My mother did not share his enthusiasm over his license. She was concerned that he might drive like my father. My father, however, was looking forward to passing on his duties as the family taxi driver. Once my brother passed his driver's exam, he scraped together enough money to purchase a used car. The car he chose was a Toyota Celica, and its maroon-colored paint was badly faded now resembling a dark shade of pink. This pink hue was quickly covered by my brother with a few cans of black primer spray paint.

After he finished spraying the car, he stood back, placed his hands on his hips, and with a large smile on his face pridefully gazed at his work. Without hesitation, I blurted out, "It looked better before you painted it!" Hearing my sarcasm, he grimaced, picked up the spray paint can, and promptly threw it toward my head. My immaturity and lack of understanding about human emotions kept me from the knowledge that unsolicited honesty can sometimes provoke a negative response. My statement caused me to suffer the injury of a black eye from the impact of the can. I now know that when making disruptive remarks, it is best to immediately follow up with an encouraging comment, if a favorable outcome is desired.

As a newly licensed driver, my brother was awarded many assignments. With his driving privilege, he inherited my father's recently vacated position as my chauffeur and the family errand boy. His new duties began to dilute his view of driving being a privilege and question whether it was more just a responsibility. If he had the foresight at the time, he could have made a good business out of picking up groceries for the other neighborhood parents.

My brother soon learned that the expense of car ownership would require him to obtain employment. He applied for a part-time job as a disc jockey at the local hangout, a skating rink called Skate World. One of the main benefits of working at the rink was that he and his family were allowed to skate for free. To his delight and my obvious approval, he was hired for the position. Because he was my new chauffeur, I not only received free transportation to the skating rink, but now I was also able to skate for free. Turns out I had nothing to be jealous of when my brother received his license, as I benefited more than he did.

Since the skating rink was indoors, free, and out of the rain, I was there every weekend. Though there were other reasons I enjoyed the skating rink, such as the slow skating sessions. To impress the girls, I invested my allowance into building the best speed skates I could afford. The internet wasn't invented yet, so putting together the best skates meant driving all around the city to find the right parts. To me it was worth the time and effort, especially since I didn't have to drive. I took a lot of pride in the skates I built; mine had bright orange wheels and green laces, the brighter the better. I loved my skates, during the winter I never took them off; they were practically glued to my feet. I was finally able to give them a rest in the summer as the weather made other activities possible.

BERRIES

When the rain subsided, I abandoned the skating rink for the great outdoors. My older brother and I were hardly ever at home. My parents owned one television which received only a few channels and had no remote control. This was the day and age when bank checks were still used to buy groceries. Writing in cursive and driving manual transmission cars was still common. Therefore, we were lucky the TV picture was even in color as at the time we did not possess the luxuries of an automatic dishwasher, microwave oven or a mobile phone. The television was mainly used for watching Saturday night wrestling and Sunday morning cartoons, and of course for playing Frogger when it came out on Nintendo.

Riding bicycles and motorcycles were my outdoor summertime passions. My older brother preferred riding motorcycles over skating, but as a hobby it was much more expensive—although after experiencing the discovery of how costly a girlfriend could be, the expense of a motorcycle didn't seem that bad to him.

During the summer months, picking berries became the resolution to the problem of the lack of funds for our hobbies. Berry fields were abundant in Oregon, and the owners of the fields would pay anyone, regardless of age, to work in the fields picking berries. There were raspberries, blackberries, and strawberry fields to choose from. Upon arrival at the field, we would pick up empty pallets and turn them in to be weighed once they were full. Field owners paid by the weight of each full pallet of berries. Since they paid by the weight, my older brother would place rocks at the bottom of the pallet before turning them in. The rocks would make the pallet heavier, so that he would get paid more.

In the berry fields, if we weren't putting rocks at the bottom of our pallets, we would be having a berry fight or gorging on handfuls of fresh berries. Like a good snowball fight, there is nothing like the exhilarating feeling of a good berry fight. I lack the ability to properly describe the taste of fresh-off-the-vine Oregon berries, and I don't believe any description would do them justice. The taste is one that you can never forget; to me the flavor is better than any sugar-filled candy a company can produce. I miss being able to consume wild berries until I could hardly move, and then drinking clean, pure refreshing water straight from a garden hose.

The Oregon blackberries were the best but accessing them risked injury as blackberry bushes were thick with thorns. Like all good things, there was work and risk involved in getting quality. Store-bought berries are easier to obtain, and preservatives provide a more appealing appearance, but the taste does not compare to that of a farm-fresh berry. It's no wonder why squirrels steal them. This is how I learned that just because something looks better doesn't mean that it is. Thankfully, because of my childhood, I can look back and remember the sweet taste of life before it changed and evolved into what it is today.

GRANDMA

The hazard presented by a berry bush thorn was no comparison to the danger of riding in a car with my father. Like in a car accident, if he was injured by a thorn, he wouldn't express his discomfort. Unlike his mother, I don't recall seeing my father ever showing any real emotion. That is not to say he wasn't stern with us when he felt it was needed. Though even while dishing out punishment to us for our misbehaviors, his mannerism never changed. You could tell he took no joy in the process. His go-to behavior adjustment tool was a track from our hot wheel toy set applied firmly to our buttocks. The use of the hot wheel track resulted in our immediate corrective reaction. I don't know if he would have achieved the same result had he instead verbally advised us of our mistake. He held the belief that sometimes action is required to procure a favorable response.

As a boy my father was taught men were not to show emotion. This would have been something that came from my grandfather as my grandmother was full of love and joy. Even upon my grandmother's passing, I never saw my father shed a tear. I don't agree with this concept that men should not show emotion. I do, though, believe that a child needs a father to teach them how to be strong. My grandfather may not have been the best father, but his complementary relationship with my grandmother made my father a good man. My grandparents' relationship and my parents' teachings led me to believe that during adolescence, a child benefits from having both a mother and a father to learn from.

My grandmother was an incredible woman, always smiling and full of life. Her presence exuded positive energy. She was anything but selfish; she saw the world from a different perspective. To her there was nothing more valuable than a person's smile, and helping others gave her purpose. I would keep a good joke ready for her in my attempts to make her smile, as she did me. She was an amazing cook; she would greet me by handing me one of her fresh-baked cookies and saying, "What a beautiful young man." I was grateful for her loving compliments and tasty treats.

Her caring nature made being sick from a cold a gift when she was there with a cup of her homemade soup. I have yet to experience any medication as emotionally healing as a genuine smile from someone you love. She taught me that in life, helping others provides us with purpose, and people need a purpose to live more than they need money. Spending time with my grandmother made me question many things in life. It made me wonder how anyone could get more enjoyment from having more houses than they could live in or more cars than they could drive, rather than making others smile.

Later in life I would read a story that caused me to reminisce over the lessons my grandmother had taught me in my youth. The story was of a man who had taken his own life by jumping off the Golden Gate Bridge in San Francisco, California. During their investigation, the police had found a letter at the man's home. The letter reportedly said that if only one person smiled at him, while he was on his walk to the bridge, he would not jump. This story, for me, really brought to light the importance of kindness to others.

After my grandfather passed, my grandmother gradually became forgetful, and my father's siblings took her in. Even in her rapid decline she remained cheerful, never becoming bitter or resentful. She loved to see people happy and provided everyone with compliments all the way till her last days. My father relayed a story of her last attempt to make her family smile for her. He stated that days before she passed, while lying in her hospital bed, my grandmother looked up at her kids and said, "It's just like my favorite soap opera show, *All My Children*." At the time she couldn't even remember my name, so I don't know how she could have possessed the cognitive ability to come up with that.

Both my parents' and my grandparents' values were securely anchored in their religious beliefs, but mine never were. My mom used to call me Doubting Thomas, as they believed in heaven and hell while I questioned the existence of these places. Although they eventually won me over and I did come to believe in God. I thought since the chances of us existing were less than that of winning the lottery, it seemed the only reasonable way to explain our creation.

My grandmother's death gave me many unanswered questions. The absence of her positive energy left me with the feeling of something missing, like the empty space left by a lost puzzle piece. Since my mom was good with puzzles, in moments like these I would usually look at her to fill in the missing pieces. This time, though, she did not have the answers to all my questions. I would ask if my grandmother was right, and what if we were all here only to help each other? Do those enriching themselves utilizing the energy of others carry more responsibility? Is hell just an eternity spent in the bad energy of others we failed in life? I now had more questions about life and death than my mom had answers for.

BELIEFS

Upon the passing of my grandmother, my five aunts confiscated her remaining assets for themselves, which included my father's small inheritance. I was never close to my aunts or cousins on my father's side and did not actually meet them until I was a teenager living in California. Though after meeting them, I found my aunts to be entitled and not family orientated, and they raised their children with the same materialistic priorities. They allowed money to establish their identity and define who they were. Their actions showed me how money possessed the ability to separate families. Because of the lessons I was provided in my childhood, it was difficult for me to grasp the concept of money becoming more important than family.

Witnessing my parents fight their fatigue to earn a living and support their family showed me the definition of financial responsibility. While contending with the difficulties of meeting their obligations, they remained grateful for the health of their family and having gainful employment. I also had the desire for the material things money could buy, but my aunts' actions, my grandma's beliefs, and my parents' struggles helped me see their lack of importance.

My mother enjoyed her work as an accountant and still to this day processes private tax returns. She loves to help show people how life can be more fulfilling by working for themselves instead of others. Learning from my parents' values caused me to contemplate the reason people were originally convinced to work for others. It was obviously derived from a need for food and shelter to survive. Though my childish mind was still too naïve to understand the depth of these hardships.

In my youthful and somewhat delusional view of how the world should be, I thought we should all be working together to meet our needs. To me, it appeared as if some people did all the work while others collected the profit. Upon bringing this question to my mother, she would explain, "Too many consumers and not enough producers." Like many of my father's statements, at the time this made no sense to me. It wasn't long before I was set straight, learning of established capitalism's ability to control the modern society's economy by creating competition.

My father had a more defiant stance on wealth, or what he called an imbalance established by the ego-driven self-righteous. He once stated to me, "The greed of man created financial separation among people, which led to the development of classes and spawned the false idols we now call stars." His views were a bit much for me to comprehend when I was younger, but I took from this statement what I could. I gathered that this was an attempt by him to tell me not to be greedy.

He would often make odd statements that I never completely understood. He told me that if you were alive before the year 1900 and you were not rich, your chances of survival were extremely low. It's possible he was trying to demonstrate how life could always be more difficult, or maybe he was just saying be glad you weren't born in 1900; I'm still not sure about that one. I do know that he believed we all had a maker who provided each of us with an expiration date. He said, "the reason we will not live forever on this earth is an attempt to limit the destructive impact of human greed on future generations."

Statements like these would make me shy away from joining him on his public outings. Once I made the mistake of visiting a used car sales lot with him. While searching for an economical car, he presented me and the salesman with yet another puzzling statement. He exclaimed, "The industrializing of America created inequality in men!" His statement was confusing to me as well as the salesman. After all, we were at a car lot, so he was not against the invention of automobiles, and he certainly loved old cars.

He had owned several different cars while living in Oregon and shared his love of cars with his sons. I think he was possibly just irritated at not being able to afford the car he wanted at the time. He may have also been feeling the pressure placed on those who lacked the ability to access what they desired. I could see how sharing an environment with those of greater means might easily cause people seeking the same to incur unwanted debt.

CHAPTER TWO

Ages 11 to 15

Surrounded by Oregon's abundant natural wonders, my father became fond of the outdoors. Organic foods like fresh vegetables, venison, and homemade ice cream were his staples. His love for nature though, did not detract from his desire to go fast; he had a passion for old cars and motorcycles. He introduced me and my brothers to motorbikes and racing at a very young age. Flat track motorcycle racing was the popular sport where I grew up. He liked the sport so much that he purchased each one of us a race bike and matching leather jackets.

At the age of eleven I received my first motorcycle. It was a used Honda 80cc dirt bike. My father had to modify the seat so that my feet would reach the ground. The seat was green as that was the cheapest material he could find; so, we painted the gas tank to match the seat and called it the Green Machine. My brother, four years older than me, had a motorcycle with a brown tank that we nicknamed the Brown Clown. I can still picture my father yelling at my brother from the side of the racetrack, "Take them down, Brown

Clown!" His statement was easily misconstrued as racist and drew many scrutinizing looks from perturbed spectators. Noticing this, my father commented that their reaction developed from a fragile mindset.

An amateur garage mechanic, my father could never leave our bikes in their original condition. Determined to give us an added advantage, it was essential for him to constantly adjust something on our bikes. On general principle he would upgrade each bike with hotter spark plugs, larger carburetors, and higher-octane fuels. He held the firm belief that real men worked with their hands, and he would often make derogatory remarks toward entertainers, whom he felt contributed nothing to society. I didn't agree with this point of view; I always enjoyed rock music and comedy-based movies.

His sustained perseverance in the development of our dirt bikes caused them to become hazardous, requiring courage and lots of practice to ride them. Of course, at that age we felt invincible enough to ride almost anything, but my father made us practice anyway. Our backyard was just over one acre, and it didn't take long for us to turn this large unused space into a practice track. We rode our motorcycles around it until a perfect circle was dug into the ground. The neighbors were not very appreciative of our track, but it was certainly entertaining for us.

We made ramps and jumps from anything we would find lying around. If it was in our way, it was run over, including bushes, toys, and even the poor dog a couple of times—unintentionally, of course. The dog, though, was twice our size, and the collision would more often hurt us and not him. Still today when I see the prices of hot wheel cars, I think of how many are buried under tire tracks in that backyard. Finally, my father decided that we had outgrown the yard, and it was time to go racing on a real track. He may also have become tired of the neighbors' complaints and having his yard torn up.

My father purchased a small trailer to tow behind his old truck that could carry our race bikes. He then located a few amateur racetracks not too far from our home where we could start our racing careers. With the time he invested in working on our bikes, it was difficult to tell if to him whether this was just a hobby or an attempt at preparing us for a future in racing. It wasn't till later in life when I saw my son win his first trophy that I realized why he invested so much in our bikes. The only feeling better than winning is watching your child win. A loving parent will gift their children with pieces of themselves until they have nothing left to give. In turn, children can provide parents with motivation and purpose when life gets difficult.

On my first race, my father assisted me by starting my bike and pushing me to the starting line. Sitting on the bike after his experimental improvements was very unsettling. Feeling the bike's power under me made me apprehensive. I told him I was scared, to which he replied, "The only way to get over fear is to tackle it." As usual I found his facetious vocabulary confusing; everyone knows the word "tackle" was reserved for fishing and football. Also, I wasn't sure how he expected me to tackle a dirt racetrack.

The roar of the bikes lining up next to me quickly brought my thoughts into focus. While placing his hand on my lower back and pushing me forward, my father offered his last words of advice: he said, "Sit closer to the gas tank to keep the front wheel from coming off the ground." I took his comment as another of one of his clever remarks and did not view it as a warning. After ignoring his essential words of wisdom, I was all ready to go. I firmly held in the clutch, put the bike into gear, and began twisting back on the throttle.

The one thing I didn't account for was the distraction provided by the overwhelming engine noise from the bikes lined up next to me. The noise grew so loud that I couldn't hear the motor on my own bike, making me unaware that I had pulled back too far on the bike's throttle. The green flag dropped, and I let out the clutch. I felt the bike lurch forward as the front wheel shot straight into the air like a rocket ship. I went from horizontal to vertical, faster than my miniature manhood could, while studying a *Playboy* magazine centerfold. My hands unconsciously reacted to the bike's forward motion by tightly squeezing down on the bike's grips.

Now having control over the handlebars didn't matter much, as the front wheel was still in the air and the bike was still moving. I had slid all the way to the back of the seat and was now almost lying on it. The back tire tore a rut into the soil which caused the bike to suddenly twist to the left. I was now being propelled straight toward the flag man and the trophy table. My mind was racing and analyzing all the damage I could cause if I crashed into the table. After sliding back to the rear fender, my legs were dangling in the air behind me. All I needed was a cape and I could finally earn the name of Superman or in my case Superboy.

Thanks to my father's advice, I pulled myself forward and was able to stay on the bike. I gained control halfway through the middle of the track, defeated gravity, and got the front wheel back on to the ground. I somehow avoided hitting the flag man, who was now running for his life, and barely missed the trophy table. Not knowing what position I was in, I continued around the track with the other racers until I saw the checkered flag. With my helmet on and being so focused on finishing the race, I didn't notice that the entire grandstand audience was standing and cheering me on, yelling "Ride 'em cowboy!" Although I did not win the race, I ended up at least completing it, to the local crowd's approval.

After the race, the flag man pulled my father aside had a talk with him about turning down the power on my bike. That day I learned that life is not always about winning the race, it's sometimes just about keeping things under control when everything goes up in the air. I also gained the knowledge that there is, obviously, such a thing as too much power.

TROPHY

Fortunately for my older brother, he was much better at riding motorcycles than I was. This was made evident by the number of trophies he had earned from his wins. His collection was a thing of pride for him but made me somewhat envious. The largest trophy in his collection stood about four feet tall. It was blue and had a shiny chrome motorbike on the top. In the middle of the trophy stood a tiny, four-inch girl with wings. To me she was the angel representing success, and from the day he won it, I couldn't take my eyes off her.

One day, I gathered the courage to ask him if I could bring the trophy with me to school for Show and Tell. This was an event where students would bring items to school to show to the other kids. Many students brought items of their own that they were proud of, but some would bring things from their parents or siblings. With a little convincing from my mother, he said, "Yes, as long as you are careful with it, and you do not tell anyone that the trophy is yours." The "careful" part I was okay with; it was the "do not tell anyone that the trophy is yours" part that I had trouble with.

Though I had another issue; I was not allowed to participate in the Show and Tell, until I brought my grades up. The elementary school I attended in Gresham was newly constructed. The school had state-of-the-art features and experienced teachers. This was a school operated by teachers with years of wisdom, attended by children too young and naïve to benefit from the advantages provided to them. When the school was constructed, the teachers with the most seniority were offered the chance to transfer here. These teachers brought with them their old school ways, like the tradition of Show and Tell.

My immaturity kept me from recognizing this educational opportunity because I had nothing to compare it with, which is often the case in life. I preferred to be outside on the playground, rather than be inside sitting at a desk, listening to a teacher talk about subjects I had no interest in. My attitude toward school provided one of my teachers with a reason to believe that I may have a learning disability. Though my mother quickly helped cure the situation by explaining to me that I would be held back a year if I did not complete the class work assignments.

The realization of my consequences of not performing was motivation enough for me. I didn't want to be held back, so I decided to enter the school's annual book reading contest. It was Thanksgiving, so the participants were instructed to make a paper turkey and place a feather on the turkey for every book they read. To prove you read the book, for each attached feather the student was required to give a brief synopsis in front of the class. I was determined to win the contest and stayed up many nights reading. This also made me accustomed to the uncomfortable feeling of speaking in front of my classmates.

The entire Hardy Boys and Nancy Drew series was my starting point. I then read some Mark Twain and of course *Pinocchio*. My favorite was *Charlotte's Web*; I was impressed by the author's imagination. It made me curious as to how this author developed such creativity, enabling them to write a book about a conversation between a pig and a spider. My guess was that this ability may have developed for them in childhood, possibly as a method of escaping from reality. These writers using books as a positive outlet in expressing themselves drew me in and caused my interest to flourish. I became determined to win, and by the time the contest ended, I had the largest paper turkey ever submitted.

After I turned in my turkey and regained the trust of my teacher, I was allowed to participate in the Show and Tell. It was finally time to bring my brother's shiny blue trophy to school. Sadly, as I expected I would, as soon as the first kid asked if I'd won it, I replied "yes." I knew it was a mistake the second the word left my lips. Within hours, the whole fifth-grade class was under the impression that I had won the trophy. I didn't know how to tell my brother that I had lied about winning the trophy, but I knew I would not escape his rath. The same could not be said of my friend Cary. He was anxious to help explain the story to my brother. On the walk home from school, Cary convinced me that he was the right one to tell my brother about the incident, so I left my fate in his hands.

As soon as we walked in the front door of my house, Cary exclaimed to my brother, "Clark lied about the trophy." I knew immediately that letting him tell my brother was yet another mistake in my series of missteps that day. Allowing someone else to tell your story will never end with a favorable result; the only person that can tell your story the way it should be told is you. The look on my brother's face demonstrated to me that it was a good time to go for a ride on my bike. As Cary finished explaining the details of my lie to my brother, I slipped out the front door, hoping to escape his outburst of anger.

Upon her arrival home, before she could even successfully manipulate our front door, my brother promptly informed my mother about my lack of honesty regarding his trophy. I was then advised by her on how I would make amends for my misstatement of facts. The next day at school I was to announce to my classmates that the trophy was indeed not mine. Lucky for me I was already used to talking in front of my class. I of course complied with my mother's request and was completely embarrassed by the incident; it would have been much easier for me to have simply told the truth in the first place. This was to be my childhood lesson in the importance of honesty.

MOTHER

At this point I was all too familiar with receiving valuable life lessons, and now understood that the purpose of childhood was to learn and grow. Surviving nature's elements may have taught me the most about respecting life. The natural setting I grew up in revealed to me how our actions had a direct impact on our environment, and the lives of those around us. As an adult while living in Southern California, I realized how lucky I was to have this exposure in my youth. I thought that maybe if some of the people I encountered here had experienced nature as I had, they might have more appreciation for the lives of others.

Mother Nature had a lot in common with my own mother when it came to life lessons. They both had an amazing method of keeping the zealous human spirit under control. My mother would say, "Nature has a way of quieting the destructive noise of our internal struggles." She seemed to have a unique view straight into the human soul, or at least it seems she did mine. I believe her inner peace and respect for life came directly from her experiences with nature.

Years after we moved to California, her favorite place to visit became a lake on the border of Arizona named Lake Powell. The lake is very large and deep; it takes several days for a boat to cross its full length. On days of nice weather, the water here is so flat it resembles glass, and in its reflection, you can see the sky above. There are several marinas on the lake that offer boats for rent. Once he discovered the boat rentals, my father saved up some money and rented a houseboat for a vacation trip. The lake was an eight-hour drive from our home in California, which my mother seemed to enjoy. The route we drove was directly through an area called the painted rocks. This area earned its name because of the large rock formations on the side of the road that had a rainbow-colored appearance. The drive was beautiful, and it was easy to see why she enjoyed it.

Spending a week at this lake with her family brought a peace and tranquility to her that I had never seen before. While driving to the lake, my father had secretly purchased some large fireworks from a roadside vender as a surprise for my mother. On the final day of the trip, my father lit off the fireworks over the lake from the back of the boat. The reflection of the fireworks off the water produced an incredible effect. It created an amazing three-dimensional spectacle of glimmering multicolored light. Sitting at the back of the boat, my mother's eyes welled up with tears as she scanned the scene before her.

The look on her face turned to sadness as we departed for home. After traveling a long way in one direction, the return trip always seems more difficult. I had previously thought this was due to the amount of energy being exerted while getting to the destination. But my mother explained that the difficulty comes from traveling in the opposite direction of where we want to be. I asked her to help explain this to me, and she replied, "Life's experiences are not meant to last forever; that's why we have memories." She then said, "There before the grace of God go I." This is her favorite saying. When I first heard her say it, I thought it meant that we shouldn't judge others because we don't know their difficulties in life. Though she explained to me that it meant we should be thankful for the abilities we have that allow us to enjoy life.

A good example of my mother's insight was how she quelled my brother's anger at me when I claimed his trophy was mine. She told him that he should see the pride I had in his success and not just the lie I told. She possessed the rare ability to pick out the good in people; she knew that it was easier to notice just the bad. That is the one lesson I struggle with; I am still not always able to look past the bad things people do. I have a difficult time perceiving if it is the person's nature or just their struggles causing their bad behavior. Though from my observation, I am not the only one that has difficulty seeing others as they truly are.

MOUNTAIN

Somedays I still struggle to employ the lessons my mother taught me. Not fully retaining what she had shown me about life meant repeating my mistakes. In my case, repeating mistakes was prevalent throughout my childhood. Like most children, I was more interested in creating chaos than paying attention to instructions. Though to my credit, chaos is a method used by nature to both teach and create, and retention appears best achieved with lessons learned through chaos.

The best lesson on how nature creates through chaos was brought to my childhood through witnessing the explosion of a large volcano. Mount Saint Helens was a volcano in the state of Washington about an hour's drive from our Oregon home. The mountain was many miles away, but it was so large it could be clearly seen from my front yard. One summer day, just after I was let out of school, this large volcano decided to erupt, turning the mountain into rubble. The volcano's eruption permanently changed the lives of thousands of residents.

On the day it exploded, May 18, 1980, several warning broadcasts were provided by the local news stations. Upon hearing the announcements, I asked my father if we should climb onto the roof of the house. My father, with a confused look on his face, turned to me and asked me "why." I replied, "To prevent being sucked into the lava flows." My father laughed and said, "It's not that kind of volcano. The mountain is a long way away in Washington, and this kind of volcano only creates ash and debris." I didn't know any better; my knowledge of volcanoes came from movies I had seen.

While the announcements were being made, local law enforcement began to evacuate inhabitants living near the mountain. Stores' shelves were emptied by citizens stocking up on supplies. Anyone just outside the blast radius, such as my family, was asked to stay inside. City employees handed out face masks and cleared the streets of cars and pedestrians.

The main eruption did not occur until hours after the warnings were given. Mother Nature always seems to provide some sign of an impending disaster, providing time to escape danger, if we pay attention. When the eruption finally took place, it was extremely violent, throwing tons of rock and ash into the air. It could be seen and heard from all over the states of Oregon and Washington. Half of the mountain was blown upward, leaving a large crater on one side. The plume of volcanic ash that filled the distant sky resembled the photograph of a nuclear bomb going off. Access roads to the mountain disappeared under all the debris. This caused the mountain to be inescapable for those who had not already left its immediate vicinity.

Ash from the mountain settled over everything, including cars, houses, trees, and roads. It floated to the ground like snow, although it didn't act like snow, we couldn't play in it, and it wouldn't melt away. The front yard of our house was blanketed in this grey colored powder with small black specs. It had the consistency of baby powder and gave the appearance of staring at a black-and-white television screen. It was difficult to understand how this debris was once part of a mountain.

My father's truck, parked in the driveway, was now unrecognizable. Since we were told not to go outside without a face mask and we had no eye protection, my brothers and I resorted to wearing our full-face motorcycle helmets. Walking in our front yard wearing our helmets, with all the ash surrounding us, we resembled astronauts roaming a distant planet. The debris remained for some time and eventually had to be removed from the street by machines. For several weeks after the explosion, city employees in street-sweeping trucks could be seen driving up and down the roads removing the debris.

Cleaning up of the volcano's remaining debris created employment opportunities that brought many out-of-town workers. The mountain's massive explosion became an international attraction. Visitors arrived from everywhere wanting to witness the devastation. Many used empty containers to collect volcanic ash from the street as souvenirs. Residents also collected the ash to sell to all the visitors. This turned out to be a great way to make extra income. In fact, my brothers and I made enough money selling ash to outsiders for us to afford to buy new bicycles. It is incredible and unexpected how nature provides for our needs.

FLIGHT

Eventually, the rain came and washed all the ash away. Schools reopened, and life started to get back to normal. Stories of the damage to the mountain were heard in every conversation for months after the incident. Visitors and news crews from around the world could still be seen taking pictures and giving tours. The presence of the television news aircraft piqued my curiosity about airplanes and flying. Ironically, I had a friend that lived only a few houses away whose grandfather owned a small plane.

One day after school while talking to my friend, Ted, he stated that his grandfather was giving visitors rides to the volcano's crater in his plane. Ted told me that his grandfather would take us for a ride if we wanted to go. Before I had a chance to ask my parents, I exclaimed, "Yes!" After arriving home, I begged them to let me go on the plane ride with Ted, and to my surprise, they agreed. I advised Ted of my parents' permission, he then contacted his grandfather and set our date with destiny.

On the day of the flight, I rode to the airport with Ted and his father, in his father's car. My excitement over my first plane ride quickly turned to fear as we approached a tiny four-seater plane parked on the tarmac. On the side of the small plane was painted the word "Destiny." By some crazy coincidence, this was the name Ted's grandfather chose for his plane. The expression on Ted's face indicated that I was not the only one made nervous by the size of the plane. Ted's grandfather approached, greeted us, and said, "So here she is boys—your Destiny." He paused after saying the name of the plane as if he was waiting for us to laugh, but only silence followed his announcement. The three of us just stood there staring at the plane in shock over its compact size.

After we boarded, Ted's father saw how nervous Ted was and told us, "Don't worry, boys, it's a short ride." Ted's grandfather then started the engine, and I could see Ted already reaching for the vomit bag. I thought, *that's a bad sign.* We were practically sitting on top of each other, so I was really hoping he wouldn't have to use the bag. The plane's fuselage began to vibrate as the throttle was pushed forward and fuel was added to the engine. While rolling down the runway, I looked over to see that the color on Ted's face had now turned a light shade of green. Taking off from the small airport, in this tiny plane with its engine roaring, pushed my guts straight to my feet. Which concerned me as I knew it would take guts to make it through this. My stomach began to rumble, and I started thinking, *I hope Ted did not take the only vomit bag.*

Despite the tiny size of the plane and the weight of its four occupants, we were able to quickly climb to elevation, allowing the plane to level out. I let go of the death grip I had on the seat, and my stomach returned to its rightful place. To my delight, the color of Ted's face also returned to normal. I thought being this high in the air would allow me to embrace the feelings of a bird in flight, but I was wrong. A bird is in complete control of its flight, and we were trapped in a tiny aluminum can, at the mercy of Ted's grandfather.

As the plane made its way to the mountain—our destiny— I mustered up the courage to look out of the window. Peering through the plane's tiny window, the scene below changed my perspective on life. Everything appeared shrunk from that distance, objects looked like they were miniature versions of their original size. Schools, houses, stores, and baseball fields were so much smaller they gave the illusion they could fit in the palm of my hand. This made it clear to me that we are a very small part of something so much bigger.

Approaching the mountain, my aerial view allowed me to fully comprehend the extent of the damage caused by the eruption. The landscape below gradually changed; the surface began to resemble a war zone. The area was unrecognizable as earth; it was as if we were flying over a distant planet. There was not a single tree left standing on the mountain. It was like someone had swiped a broom across the mountain and laid them all down. Gray ash covered everything; roads and buildings were no longer discernable. The two lakes on the mountain were transformed into huge mud puddles, full of floating trees. Nothing could have survived this; the terrain had been completely decimated.

After flying through the massive crater caused by the explosion we made our way back to the airport. We somehow managed to survive our adventure in one piece, or at least most of us did; I believe Ted may have left his stomach somewhere over the mountain. Between what we had just witnessed and surviving the plane ride, by the time we landed there was only silence among us. Our exploration to witness this intense power provided a level of respect for Mother Nature that now felt impossible to develop toward other humans.

GIRLS

Ted and I remained friends throughout grade school, and although we would meet up later in life, I didn't see him much after that. Things changed for me when I started middle school: life became more about meeting girls. The middle school I attended was named Gordon Russell after a local family patriarch, said to be an Olympic wrestler. It was state of the art in 1980. Every kid in the area wanted to attend this school, and I was just lucky enough to be in the correct zip code. The kids at this school were very Intune with the current clothing trends; every day was a fashion show. Bell-bottom pants were not in style anymore; for boys it was now Nike brand shoes and tight-legged jeans. Personally, I was glad that bell bottoms were no longer a fad because they always got caught in my bicycle chain.

My parents had a difficult time keeping up financially with the cost of clothing trends. Before I left for the bus stop in the morning, I would watch my mom dig in her purse to try and find spare change for my lunch. Due to our lack of wealth, government cheese and packaged noodles became staples of our diet. Meals consisting of cheese sandwiches and instant soup were common in my household. Not knowing any better, my brothers and I found this food delicious.

My wish was to participate in sports at my new school, but discovered I was too small for football and too short for basketball, so I chose wrestling. The fact that the school was built on the reputation of wrestlers also suited my athletic decision. Turns out it was the right fit; I won several tournaments. I wrestled for only two years and quit mainly because I didn't enjoy wearing the required wrestling uniform. The outfit was basically a single-strap leotard that was uncomfortable, and not very attractive. It was less than flattering to my undeveloped physique. This was not helpful with making me appear desirable to female spectators, and at that age I felt I could use all the help I could get. Besides, I still had roller skating and bike riding as hobbies.

Skating remained an activity for me even after I entered middle school, and why not? My admission was free, and it was an easy way to meet girls. All I had to do was ask them to slow skate with me, sooner or later one of them would say yes; the odds were on my side. It also didn't hurt that my brother worked at the rink, and the girls saw that I had free entry.

Weekends were my favorite time to go skating. On one Saturday night at the skating rink, while in line at the snack bar, I glanced over and noticed the most impossibly radiant vision of beauty. Her incredible smile, long flowing blond hair, and ability to skate made her the complete package. When I first saw her, she was rolling around the rink on a pair of shimmering pink skates. At the time I had a peculiar imagination and watching her reminded me of the exhilaration I felt while catching my first fish on a new lure. To me she represented a shiny, pink-colored jig skimming across the water, and I was the mesmerized fish racing upstream after it. I was hooked the second I saw her; I had taken the bait and was ready to be reeled all the way in.

While staring at her, my mouth dropped open, and my eyes widened. With this vacant look on my face, I must have truly resembled a fish in pursuit of a lure. I leaped over the rope at the snack bar line and made my way up to the disc jockey booth, where my brother was working. I grasped onto his shoulder and whispered in his ear, "You need to announce a slow skate." He saw that I was staring at the girl, smiled and nodded his head in agreement, then dimmed the lights on the skating rink floor.

The song "Open Arms" by the rock music group Journey began to play as the slow skate was announced. It was the perfect song for the moment, and it was time for me to make my big move. I gathered all my confidence and made my way over to her. I was nervous but I thought if I never ask the question, I will never know the answer. I proceeded to ask her if she wanted to slow skate with me, and to my great relief, she smiled and replied, "Yes."

Letting out all the air I had built up in my lungs from holding my breath, I took her by the hand and headed to the skate floor. Her hand was soft, warm, and comfortable; it was like wearing the perfect fitting glove. I was sweating profusely, but regardless, I wasn't about to let go of her. This new feeling was strange and wonderful, but also just a little scary. It was the first time I felt that way and for me that was it; I was smitten.

CHAPTER THREE

Ages 15 and 16

The girl from the rink was named Tawnya, and she was to be my first girlfriend. Her beauty demanded the attention of other boys in her vicinity. She was gifted with appealing looks and an outgoing personality; I was proud to be with her. I thought that she was perfect for me, but I may not have been the right fit for her. We had our differences; she had not grown up as I did. She was provided with an opulent life, due to her affluent parents. Though, at the time, to me anyone with an inground pool in their backyard was wealthy. I wanted so much for her to like me that I tried not to bring up the dissimilarities in our lifestyles.

We enjoyed walking home together from the skating rink, hand in hand. On our walks we occasionally stopped by our favorite local ice cream shop, named Dea's. There was nothing better than holding Tawnya's hand and walking to get ice cream on a warm summer day. The ice cream cones at Dea's were the best in town. I could hardly wait to taste one, although I would usually lose half of it as it melted and dripped on to the ground. Wiping the melted ice cream from my hand meant letting go of Tawnya's, and I would rather just let the ice cream drip onto the floor.

The back area of the ice cream shop had video games, where we would meet up with our friends. One kid named Chad, whom I knew from school, was always hanging out there. Chad was a mean-spirited kid, who seemed to take enjoyment from making rude comments to girls. Tawnya said that it was just immaturity, though I thought it was more likely insecurity. Chad did not have a good role model in his life. His father was mean to him; always yelling at him. His father was an avid hunter, like mine, but he liked to kill animals for sport, mine would only kill animals for food. I personally never understood the killing of animals for sport, when I asked about this my father replied, "to each his own."

One afternoon on our walk home from getting ice cream, I noticed that Chad had begun to follow us. Uncertain of his intentions, I squeezed Tawnya's hand in mine, pulled her closer to me, and quickened our pace. Chad caught up to us and immediately started saying rude things about Tawnya. He asked her if she got her big butt from her mom and where her pink skates were. Tawnya responded to him by saying, "Shut up and go home Chad."

Chad's aggressive tone gave me cause to be concerned, and I began to look for a possible escape route. I saw only a trench designed to carry rainwater on one side of us, and the road on the other side. Just as I started to guide Tawnya across the street, Chad unexpectedly grabbed her by the shoulders, pushed her into the trench and jumped on top of her. I was shocked by his actions; I really didn't think that his verbal assaults would turn physical.

Knowing she could be hurt by his assault; I didn't hesitate in jumping on his back to pull him off her. Unfortunately, he was much bigger than me and was able to simply push me away. Chad was now straddling Tawnya while she was hitting him and yelling "get off me." Her actions seemed to fuel his aggression toward her. I thought about getting a rock to hit him with, but there were none within my reach. There was no one else around to help, so I had to quickly figure out another way to remove him. Since the method my father would use, of getting a rock, wasn't available, I thought I could instead try one my mother might deploy. I asked Chad to please get off her, but he of course just ignored my request.

My parents' methods had failed, and I was becoming frustrated watching Tawnya struggle. I then realized I could get him off her if I could somehow trade places with him, like I would in a wrestling move. I clasped onto his shoulder with my hand and yelled, "Hey, she's my girlfriend I'm first!" Bewildered by my comment, he released his hold and dismounted her. Seeing this I immediately moved toward her and acted as if I was going to take his place on top of her. Instead, I grasped onto her arms and pulled her to her feet. I placed my back toward Chad, looked Tawnya in her eyes, and told her to run.

As Tawnya began to run away, I turned around to see that Chad was visibly very upset, he screamed in my face "Why did you do that?" He obviously didn't realize that he had just been tricked. There was nothing left for me to say, so I didn't answer him, I just turned and walked away. Tawnya made it safely to my house, and I arrived shortly after. To my dismay, she did not seem happy to see me. She just asked me not to tell her father about the incident. Not wanting to upset her any more than she already was, I simply agreed. I was just glad to see that she was not injured.

FAIR

The night after the incident with Chad, she formerly introduced me to her father. I found him to be of diminutive stature, possessing an overconfident, prideful persona. He did not display an inviting attitude toward me, but this didn't bother me much. I attributed his demeanor to being a protective father. During our meeting, Tawnya advised him that I had invited her to accompany me to this year's Portland State Fair. She then made the request that he provide us with transportation to which he begrudgingly agreed.

Her father owned a butcher shop and used the shop's cargo delivery van to drive us. Our unromantic ride in the back of his drab old work van, like some type of meat product, made me wish I had asked my father to shuttle us there instead. An associate of his also accompanied us and sat in the front passenger seat, while Tawnya and I rode in the van's back cargo area. His associate was a large, poorly dressed man of European descent. While enroute to the fair, I could hear her father yelling incoherently at his passenger seat companion. Their argument abruptly ended as her father dropped the man off at his meat-cutting business.

The rest of our journey was marked by silence. Arriving at the fair, Tawnya and I climbed out of the van and said goodbye to her father. Before driving off, her father remarked "I will be back to pick you up in two hours at this spot." I thought it was strange how he made us ride in the back of the van, and then berated his coworker right in front of us. I tried not to get sidetracked by this; I didn't want anything to distract me from enjoying the fair with Tawnya.

The fair was crowded, but we still had a wonderful time eating popcorn and going on carnival rides. I tried to hold her hand as much as possible so that we would not lose each other in the crowd.

At least, that was the excuse I gave her; I just enjoyed the feeling of her hand in mine. Partaking in the festivities were several large Navy ships docked along the Columbia River. The enormous battleships were conducting tours for fair attendees. This was my first experience seeing a ship of that size; much less being allowed to walk on one. The massive guns on the ships were a sight to behold. They made me curious as to how it was possible to build something like this and ponder the need for their construction.

Tawnya did not find the battleships as interesting as I did. She preferred spending time at the carnival games and small shops. One of the tents was selling jewelry, and she found a bracelet she liked. I thought this was my chance to buy her something special to remember our time here. I had saved my last twenty dollars just for a moment like this. I removed the twenty-dollar bill from my pocket and handed it to the shop vender indicating that I wanted to purchase the bracelet. She smiled as I placed the gold-colored bracelet on her wrist. It fit perfectly and was the best purchase I had made all day.

As soon as her father picked us up, Tawnya enthusiastically presented him with the gift I had bought for her. He briefly glanced at it and in his deep overbearing voice stated, "It's cheap!" Tawnya, appearing disappointed at her father's statement, frowned and looked away. I told her I was sorry about the bracelet but that I had one dollar left if she would like to split it with me, to which she replied "alright."

She loved hearts, so I drew one in the middle of the one-dollar bill and tore it in half. I then handed her one side of the bill with half the drawn heart and told her, "Now you have half my heart." She smiled at my sentimental gesture and placed the half dollar in her pocket. This was the last memento I would give to her; I was unaware that our time together was fleeting. Tawnya broke up with me the next week, informing me through a "Dear John" type of letter that she had a new boyfriend. Life has an abruptly harsh method of showing us the value of time.

This news of her breaking up with me was difficult to digest. Though after the incident with her father and the bracelet, I should not have been surprised. I saw her at the rink the next weekend, she was skating hand in hand with her new boyfriend, as we used to. I recognized him immediately; he was a frequent visitor to the rink. I was too ashamed to say anything, but what was there to say? She had made her decision. It felt like my heart had been torn from my chest, and I wished to never feel this way again.

Accepting what she saw in him was not easy for me. He not only looked dull himself but seemed to be reflecting his dullness onto her. I don't know what about him that she found more attractive, though I was sure it wasn't his looks. I thought maybe it was something to do with his maturity, as he was a year older than me. What ever it was, she obviously observed a difference in him significant enough to leave me. It wasn't until I observed him purchasing a new set of skates for her that I recognized her true motivation. To help reduce my frustration, I tried to justify her actions rather than allow bitterness and resentment to dominate my attitude.

On the way home from the rink while listening to a rock love ballad on the radio, the words in the song made me realize that I was not alone in my suffering. Unfortunately, I couldn't seek comfort from my friends, they were too inexperienced to sympathize with me. Regardless, I wouldn't be able to explain it to them. A heart makes no sound when it breaks, so how was I to explain this pain to someone that had never felt it. I decided to confide in my mother about my situation. In confronting her she tried to avoid the subject, by telling me that I should talk to my father. Forever attempting to be the scholar, when I asked him about girls, he said, "Look, son, women are who they are, you can't change them, and you can't control them any more than you can control the weather." His words were of little consolation and as usual made no sense to me.

While losing her seemed traumatic at my young age, it was yet another learning process that I had to endure. Experiences like this taught me about love, women, and the need to protect my feelings and reactions to situations out of my control. I found women to be as complicated as they are amazing; they can conceive life while destroying hearts. These beautiful creations were a wild dance of emotion, and I could not allow myself to become resentful of the pain they may unwittingly distribute.

BIKES

The sight of Tawnya at the skating rink with another boy caused me to lose interest in my roller-skating hobby. I decided I would start spending more time riding and building bicycles. My friend Cary worked at the local bicycle shop, which enabled him to get parts for our bikes at a discount. Cary was anything but sedentary; he was always going. We spent several hours every day at the bike shop, upgrading our bikes by adding better high-performance parts. Every newly installed part required us to perform a test ride on our homemade track. Cary was consumed with the process of building the best bike possible. No matter how well our bikes performed, he always wanted his to be better.

The bike shop was situated on a hilltop overlooking the city. This made the street leading up to the shop the perfect place to test the speed of our bikes. Too difficult to ride up, Cary and I would walk our bikes to the top of the hill and then race down. He would usually win, not because his bike was faster but because he had no fear. The first time we pushed our bikes up the hill, I removed my shirt, exposing a large dark birthmark that lay directly over my heart. When he saw it, Cary exclaimed, "That's how you died in your previous life!" He was always talking about death; I figured this was just part of his fearless, rebellious personality.

Hanging out with him was exciting but also frightening. He possessed a dangerous mix of intelligence and impulsiveness, without any concern for consequences. The only thing he feared was his dad, who worked as a local police officer. Cary was the living fable of the cop's son gone bad. His dad's protective behavior bordered on emotional abuse, which made Cary resentful and inspired him to seek his freedom any way possible.

He would usually spend more time at my house than his own. I thought that this was because I had a larger backyard to ride bikes in, but I learned that for him it represented a sanctuary. Although appearing random, many of his actions were purposefully aimed at getting his father's attention. He liked to brag about how he would take his dad's truck out for joyrides. Once he tried to convince me to go with him, but I was less than a year away from getting my driver's license and didn't want to take the chance. A driver's license for a kid in Oregon represented freedom and was not to be risked. Stories were frequently told of young adults losing their driving privileges before they even had their own car. I was not as fearless as Cary and was not willing to risk having my opportunity to drive taken away.

Like with Cary's, most of my friends' bikes could usually be found lying in my parents' front yard after school. My father was constantly tripping over the bikes in the front walkway of the house, though he never complained. I'm sure he was just glad he knew where we were and that we were safe. With all the activity at the house, the area was safe from bike thieves searching for crimes of opportunity.

That is, until Cary came up with the brilliant idea of stealing his own bike.

He shared a story with me, told to him by his dad, in which a kid's bike was stolen from someone's yard, and the homeowner's insurance replaced it with a new one. Cary, with all his fearless wisdom, wanted to try this himself. I told him he was crazy, as he already had a nice bike. His plan was to say he left his bike in my front yard, then disassemble it and hide it under his bed. I didn't think he was serious until he actually did it.

Within a day of him revealing his plan to me, the local police showed up at my house, asking about his missing bike. Cary told the cops that he had left the bike in front of my house as he had planned to do. With the cops questioning my parents about his bike and then my parents asking me if I knew where it was, I felt forced to lie and say, "I don't know." I was upset with Cary; he had sacrificed my honesty for his personal gain. Although I was more concerned about the wrath his father would dispense had I told the truth. I knew what he had done, and now my parents were suspicious about who stole the bike.

Sure enough, a few days later Cary showed up at my house with a brand-new bike, which he bought with the money from his father's home insurance. I asked Cary, "What did you do with the old bike?" He took me to his house and showed me: it was in pieces under his bed. I told him that if he got caught, he would lose both bikes. I then asked him, "What do you plan to do with the old bike now that it will be recognized as stolen?" He didn't have an answer; he was more curious to see if he could pull it off. I surmised from this that it is always beneficial to reevaluate any decision based on dishonesty or greed. By doing this I would hopefully be prevented from taking impulsive selfish actions that can have a negative impact on others' lives, as Cary had mine.

SCHOOL

His fraudulent bike theft made me want to avoid spending time with Cary. Instead, I concentrated on preparing for high school and taking my driver's license test. After graduating from middle school, I enrolled at Gresham High, the same school my older brother had attended. This high school had an indoor pool, an escalator, two indoor gyms, a large auditorium, and of course more girls. The school resembled a castle, with tall ceilings and hallways that stretched forever. Schools in Oregon require a larger occupiable interior space because the weather prevents an open campus.

Due to all the rain, the high school offered mainly indoor sports. Since I had wrestled in middle school, I thought I would try it again at this new school. Though, as it turned out, in high school wrestling was not as popular and even ridiculed by most students. I was impressionable at that age and desperately wanted to fit in, so I decided it was time to permanently retire my single-shoulder leotard. I loved the school's large indoor pool and wanted to join the swimming team, but that was not meant to be either. I was too embarrassed by the large birthmark on my chest to remove my shirt in front of the girls.

It was obvious I was not going to be involved in after-school sports. Therefore, I figured I would get a job so that I could start saving for a car. I applied for and obtained a part-time job at a local upholstery shop. My duties consisted of stocking rolls of fabric and vacuuming the store. The job was tedious, so I purchased a Walkman audio cassette player to keep me entertained. The cassette player helped occupy my mind and provided a distraction from my work. With every paycheck I would go next door to the record store and purchase a new rock music cassette tape. The tapes initiated me into the world of rock music, and I became addicted to the energy it supplied me with.

Although boring, my new job enabled me to afford car insurance and finally get my driver's license. My brother was very thankful after I passed my driving test because he would no longer have to drive me around town. Until I could afford to buy my own car, I was forced to drive my father's old 1973 Chevy El Camino. This was a very large vehicle and difficult to drive. The size of the car made it feel more like floating in a boat. The car was great for my accident-prone father, but not so much for a fifteen-year-old kid who didn't know how to parallel park. To make things worse It was solid black, and had no air conditioning, which led to the interior being very hot in the summer. Still, regardless of what you drove, in high school if you had a car, you were popular.

Driving, playing sports, and the ability to obtain alcoholic drinks were sources of popularity at my high school. Students who were not involved in meaningful after-school pursuits, like sports or part-time work, were left with idle time. Many filled these empty hours attempting to dissuade their hormones, by experimenting with adrenaline rendering stimulants. This was of course done in opposition and in defiance of warnings from authority figures. Pure pressure, the desire to feel accepted, made trying these substances common among many teenagers here. Like most kids I had sneaked sips of my father's whiskey, but narcotics were a new concept for me. My parents' constant preaching on the dangers of drug use made me reluctant to hang around kids, who were known to be involved in this activity.

Though it was inevitable that I would encounter a situation where I was offered some form of illegal substance. I was confronted with such an occurrence in the third week of my freshman year.

While in the school parking lot, I was approached by some friends smoking a marijuana cigarette. I began to engage in conversation with them, when one of the kids offered me the joint to smoke. This is one of those situations when I could subconsciously hear my mom's voice saying the words, "curiosity killed the cat."

The teenagers participating in smoking were trying to hide the joint as they passed it along. I could sense they were each paranoid about taking it, though they were still attempting to act like they were enjoying it. As the joint was passed to me, I now had a dilemma: by not taking the joint I would be labeled a snitch, but I was not interested in partaking in the consumption of drugs. Saying no to peer pressure takes a lot of courage; no one wants to feel the loneliness of being an outsider. When the joint was offered to me, I took it, pressed it against my lips, turned my head and acted as if I was inhaling. I now understood why the other kids felt paranoid, just holding the joint felt wrong. I quickly passed it over to the next kid and said thanks.

My assumption was that they had bought my mock inhale, because they didn't say anything about it. One of the kids in the group I recognized from my middle school; he was an Oregon state wrestling champion. When it came time for him to smoke the joint, he looked nervous, and I could sense that he didn't want to participate. Nonetheless, not wanting to lose his popularity by refusing, he succumbed to the pressure and smoked the joint. I was growing uncomfortable with the scene around me, so I stated I had to go and quickly made my exit.

The next day the local newspaper reported that one of the teenagers from the school parking lot had been involved in a bad accident. It turned out to be the wrestler, he had wrecked his motorcycle while leaving the parking lot. The news report stated that when the accident happened, he was intoxicated and not wearing a helmet. The wrestler was thrown from his bike and sustained an injury to his head, which ended up causing him permanent paralysis. A few of the other kids participating that day started to complain of feeling sick and were taken to the hospital. A subsequent police investigation showed that the joint they were smoking had been laced with some type of chemical. This close call prompted me to distance myself from those ingesting drugs and established my extremely cautious approach to taking medication.

HUNTING

Sadly, for his family, the wrestler's accident occurred just a week before Christmas. This was usually a joyous time of year; the celebration of Christmas was important to the local community. Most area families were of low income, making this holiday tradition the only time many kids received gifts. There were parades on the streets and Santa Claus actors at every shopping center, while decorative lights adorned all the area houses. I really enjoyed witnessing the transformation of the town and the spirits of the people around me.

Still in the back of everyone's mind, were the precautions required to prevent weather-related accidents and tragedies, like that of the wrestlers. My father had his own opinions of incidents occurring during this time of year, which I will not repeat, especially given his own accident record. Thinking back on it now, I believe as a parent he may have possibly felt helpless in preventing kids, like the wrestler, from becoming injured unnecessarily. He once told me that he had observed a bad accident while he was walking to school. Apparently as a kid, he had witnessed two of his classmates perish when they were hit by a truck, while crossing a road. This may have also contributed to his issues with bad drivers. His internal battles caused him frustration, which thanks to his father, he didn't know how to properly express.

For him, this time of year represented the hardships caused by the unrelenting rain and snow. He used the sport of hunting as a distraction to escape reality and as a release from his stress. That year for Christmas he purchased a rifle for me so I could hunt with him. I was excited to receive such a gift but honestly, I would have rather got a bike. Hunting was not as much of a thrill to me as it was for him.

On the way back from the "GI Joe" store, where he bought the rifle, he made another of his many remarks. In a sarcastic tone, he said, "Christmas has become too commercialized. It's all about making money, and it only teaches children they can get free stuff." The expression on my mother's face revealed that she did not appreciate his comment. Speaking loud enough for him to hear, she declared to him that this was his unresolved emotional damage from not receiving gifts as a child. She then stated, "Digging up stuff from the past and placing it on the ground doesn't mean it's alive; it's still dead, and more comfortable for everyone if left buried."

My mother often acted like a silt fence at the bottom of his eroding hill. She was catching all the sediment from his storm, preventing the pollution from causing damage to others' mental landscape. Regardless of his statements, I still loved spending time with my father in nature, except of course while hunting. His main target was big game wildlife such as deer and elk, which he found near my grandparents' farm. I could almost see the stress leave him when we entered the farms long driveway. Everyone should have an escape, a place where they feel comfortable letting go of their frustration, and for him this was their farm. The freezer in our home was always full of sausage and venison from his frequent hunting exploits.

My grandparents' farm was forty acres of dense, lush forest, about fifty miles from Gresham on the Oregon coast. Their farm was in a small town named Vernonia, which consisted of only one store and a gas station. The tranquil beauty of the area was often overshadowed by its many painful hazards. This is where I was first exposed to the thrills of hunting, the itch of poison oak, the burn of an electric cow fence, and the sting from the pinch of a crawdad claw.

Besides hunting and chores, there really wasn't much else to do for an adult this far away from society, among Oregon's heavily wooded landscape. Which is probably why much of my grandmother's daily diet consisted of a gallon of my grandfather's homemade wine. I remember the day I grew brave enough to sneak a sip of her wine, I instantly regretted this decision, it tasted like vinegar and grape juice. It was an acquired taste, and I'm guessing after years of drinking it, she likely had no taste buds left.

While preventing myself from ever becoming an alcoholic by trying her wine, my father helped to cure my older brother of smoking. My grandfather would leave his handmade cigarettes by the old wood burning stove. When no one was looking, my brother saw the chance and stole one of his cigarettes. My father caught him smoking it behind the barn and proceeded to make him smoke the remaining cigarettes in the pack. To this day my brother cannot look at a cigarette without feeling sick, and I don't like alcohol. Our disgust with my grandparents' vices became a deterrent helping to ensure our longevity.

There were two houses on their farm, one newly built by my uncle for his family and the original one occupied by my grandparents. The original home was built in 1950, it consisted of one bedroom and a living room and had only a wood-burning stove for heat. Animals were abundant on the farm, they included chickens, cows, horses, and even pigs. Some of the acreage had been cleared of trees to create my grandmother's garden. This made fresh vegetables easily accessible by simply walking out the back door and picking them.

With the garden also came varmints, rodents such as mice and squirrels were common. My grandfather primarily disliked the squirrels: he referred to them as evil destructive critters that were always pillaging and hoarding their spoils. To catch them, he would place the largest nuts and strawberries inside traps on the edges of the garden. Like squirrels, I had a fondness for fresh strawberries, although this was the only commonality I had with them.

The food from my grandparents' farm turned out to be much more gratifying to me than hunting. Hunting with my father was very boring. It amounted to hours of waiting deep in the woods for prey to show itself so that we could shoot it. Then when we finally did get a shot at a deer or an elk, there was the procedure of cutting it into sections small enough to extract it. Dressing was the next part of the hunting process and was not at all what it sounded like. I originally pictured it as simply placing a blanket over the animal carcass. As it turned out, I was badly mistaken.

Dressing was the process of removing the skin from the deer to retrieve the edible meat. The first time I witnessed my father and uncle dressing a deer, I was over the whole deer-hunting experience. Not that I wanted to be a vegetarian, but there was smaller game available that was much easier to prepare. My father and uncle weren't bothered by the process. In fact, my uncle may have enjoyed it; he was experienced in living off the land.

A lumberjack by trade, my uncle had so many scars, he could have been used as a scarecrow. One of his larger scars ran diagonally all the way across his face. While cutting a log he was struck by the blade of a chainsaw, when it kicked back after hitting a knot. I'm not sure how my aunt dealt with this lifestyle and caring for all his injuries. They never seemed to fit together as a couple; she was from the city, and he was from the country. I think it was just that she loved his wild spirit; this was the definition of the saying "opposites attract."

DOGS

Both my uncle and my father were fond of large dogs. My uncle owned several hunting dogs, or at least what he considered hunting dogs. His dogs were just strays he had picked up along the way and trained to hunt. My father also owned a couple of big dogs during my childhood. His favorite breed was the Saint Bernard. He had bought a female and named her Brandi. She was white with brown spots, weighed over two hundred pounds, and was very protective of kids.

Brandi was gentle with me and my brothers, but not as welcoming to strangers. It wasn't wise to enter our backyard if she didn't know you. She had a built-in emotional barometer and could sense danger. This may be the reason my father liked the breed; he never had to worry about the security of his family. She brought us a lot of joy and comfort. It's hard to beat hugging a big fluffy friendly dog when you are feeling down. Growing up with Brandi to rely on was like having a best friend that would never forsake you.

One of my father's favorite things to do with Brandi was to feed her leftover food scraps from under the dinner table. Having all my family, along with Brandi, gathered to enjoy the farm fresh food, made my grandmother's the place to be for the holidays. Fresh vegetables from my grandmother's garden, accompanied by venison, were commonplace meals at our dinner table. All the food from my grandparents' farm was fresh, whether it was vegetables, venison, chicken noodle soup from farm-raised chickens and hand-rolled noodles, or freshly made ice cream.

To this day, I can still recall the taste of the food from my grandmother's farm. I haven't experienced anything quite like it since. I never bothered to share this information with my friends as I got older, I knew my description would not do it justice. It's not unlike going to Disneyland for the first time. You can describe a six-foot mouse to someone, but you can't share how you feel about it. Sense, like taste, are personal. Maybe this is why doctors have so many misdiagnoses; they must rely on the patient's description. Brandi showed that this was equally important when it came to pets. We must pay close attention to them, because they cannot voice the exact location of their discomfort.

Anyone who has owned a pet knows that the hardest part is when their time is up, and you have to say goodbye. The life of a pet is so short that we must make the best of it while they are here. My father knew this well and treated Brandi like a queen until she grew old and passed away. Having pets when I was younger taught me how precious and valuable time is. I now try to be more appreciative of others' time, as they are sharing with me their most valuable asset.

CHAPTER FOUR

Ages 16 to 25

It was nice to see how hunting allowed my father a break from his daily routine. He worked long hours, which kept him from his family and was tough on him physically. I knew he desired a change and that he wanted to see more of his siblings in California. It wasn't long before his words turned into action. One day after he arrived home from work, he made a stunning, life-altering announcement to the family. He gathered us together, sat us all down in the living room, and stated, "I was laid off, and we are moving to California."

These were unwelcome words, and they echoed through my mind like a voice in the Grand Canyon. My younger brother was still in grade school, so my father's news did not affect him. Though the situation was not the same for me and my older brother. He had just graduated high school and was not looking forward to moving away from his friends. To this day, as an adult, he is drawn to Oregon and the place where he grew up. As for me, I knew my father's announcement would cause many traumatic changes in my life. I just started to make friends and become comfortable at my new school. I had a lot to lose, from my new high school to my job, and even a new girlfriend.

My new girlfriend was an attractive blond-haired girl. She was the same age as me and coincidentally lived in the same neighborhood. Her name was Cassidy, and she was special to me because she possessed the same likes and dislikes as me. The first time we kissed, it felt like I had been sucked into a vacuum and whisked straight to heaven. Her favorite song was "Little Red Corvette" by the artist Prince. It was a great song, though listening to it made me recall the Corvette my father had crushed with his truck. I find it puzzling why we relate tragic memories to current experiences in life. This must be the reason it becomes difficult to be open-minded when encountering new emotions that make us recall the past.

Cassidy liked Prince's song so much that I purchased her the cassette tape *Purple Rain* for her birthday. When the tape became unwound, she would give it to me to repair. She found it impressive that I could use the end of a number-two pencil to wind the tape backup. I couldn't help but notice the smile on her face every time she handed me the cassette to fix. I started to think she was pulling the tape from the cassette on purpose. This made me wonder if she was doing this for herself or for me, to make me feel more masculine. Either way, it didn't matter to me. I was happy to help, and to collect as my payment her beautiful smile when I handed back the cassette to her.

The knowledge that I would soon be forced to leave her, and that my life here would end, was difficult for me to accept. Change was inevitable, but I wasn't mentally prepared for this catastrophic adjustment in my young life. I tried to move past my sadness and lift my spirits by imagining the movie stars I might see in California. I even had that moment where I envisioned what it might be like if I were famous. I'm sure I was not the minority in this thought process; I have no doubt anyone moving to California at one time had some small dream of stardom.

My fascination with being famous was obviously fleeting. This momentary delusion of grandeur about having a career in movies was quickly quelled by my father's feelings on the subject. He remained resolute in his belief that men worked with their hands and wanted me to do the same. His goal after his arrival was to acquire a job with his brother in the construction industry. His siblings all resided in California, they included one brother and six sisters. I had never met these relatives, though I was looking forward to seeing them. All I knew about my cousins I had learned through conversations with my father.

MOVE

Moving day arrived and we left for California in a large, enclosed truck, full of my parents' furniture. I rode with my father in the moving truck, while my mother and brothers followed behind in my mother's car. It was going to be a long drive, especially for a kid. I could see that the move placed a lot of strain on my parents. Little did they know that the courage they were displaying would help me in a similar move, I would be compelled to make later in life.

While traveling toward our destination, the landscape changed dramatically. Our expedition south started in beautiful, lush green hills and descended into a barren brown desert. The target was an area an hour north of Los Angeles in Southern California. Traversing the last downhill stretch of freeway and acquiring my first glimpse at the area, it registered with me why they called it the "high desert." My father attempted to lift our spirits by saying, "Wow, boys, look at all the dirt you can ride your bikes on!" This statement reminded me of the scene from the movie *Vacation* where the character "Clark Griswold" was admiring their Christmas tree. Although unfortunately, his comment was not meant to be facetious, and by the look on my brother's face I could tell that he was also not impressed.

The terrain here was flat and desolate, with dirt as far as the eye could see. I noticed right off that all the trees were very small and oddly shaped. My mother informed me that these deformed-looking trees were a protected species known as the Joshua Tree. I told my mother, "Maybe Joshua should have watered his trees." By squinting, I could make out the shape of mountains in the far distance. Which gave me some hope of normal trees possibly becoming visible again.

My new surroundings did not distract me from the empty space left by the absence of my girlfriend. I longed for the sound of her voice; my only resolve was to try to call or write to her when we arrived. However, I knew my effort would be pointless, I was only fifteen years old and felt I now had no route back to her. My brother felt the same way about all his friends he left behind; he was old enough to go his own way but lacked the means. This is why our memories are so important. Like riding a bike, in life we must keep moving forward; no matter how much we want to relive the past, we can't go back.

Once we arrived in Southern California, my father decided it was time for us to meet the rest of his family. He planned a gathering, and everyone from his side of the family was scheduled to attend. Meeting my cousins sounded exciting, although as it turned out, only a few of them showed up, and they didn't stay long. When I did finally have a chance to meet them, they came across as very uptight and distant. I now understood why my mother did not care for them much.

:353

Knowing that we are all individuals, and therefore were supposed to have different personalities, I tried to keep an open mind. Though the more personalities I encountered in this new state, the more I started to become disappointed in our decision to move here. I became concerned as the attitude of the people in this place seemed so indifferent to the world around them. I even wondered if they were all on some type of prescription medication, as they acted estranged from reality. Although I remained hopeful that Californians were not all like my relatives.

Withdrawing from wanting to interact with others, I notice this now included limiting my contact with my father's family. I made the conscious decision not to visit them. This was possibly my attempt at avoiding the inadequate feeling they provided me with. My father was also having difficulty in his pursuit of procuring employment here, and my relatives appeared unlikely to help him. He was left to his own devices, and eventually found work with a local contractor installing garage doors on single-family homes.

Once he secured employment, he found us a place to live and enrolled me in a local high school. The school had an elongated layout, nothing like the ones in Oregon. This new school was basically a bunch of modular buildings assembled in the middle of the desert. The students here were, for the most part, not very welcoming. I discovered the reason for their unapproachable posture on the first day of my attendance, when I was offered narcotics. There appeared to be a substantial issue with the use of drugs at the school, which the teachers were obviously oblivious to. Marijuana was the students' drug of choice and was readily available here. My previous encounter with a marijuana joint made my decision to stay away from drugs much easier. Although, not participating guaranteed meeting new friends would be an arduous process.

After settling into my bizarre new high school, I found a job as a busboy for a local restaurant. My job turned out to be much more pleasant than the school was. The after-school job also helped me to stay out of trouble. To assist with my new commutes, my father helped me purchase a car. We bought the only car I could afford; it was a used orange Subaru with a manual gearbox. It was ugly, small and it didn't shift very well, but it taught me how to drive a stick shift, and it was better than walking. When buying the car, my father said, "On a busboy's wage, beggars can't be choosers."

Since the car was small, round, and orange colored, I nicknamed it Vitamin-C. I knew Vitamin-C wasn't going to be of much help to me when it came to dating girls. So, I saved every penny of my tips from my new job, to buy a different car. Once I had enough money I went shopping and found the perfect car to lift my young libido, after losing Cassidy. It was a used blue 1980 Chevy Camaro. This car completely changed my attitude on life. The car gave me confidence and inspired me to ask one of the waitresses I worked with, out on a date.

LOVE

She was irresistibly attractive and had the golden-colored hair which had now become my Kryptonite. Her name was Rose, and she was older than me by almost ten years. From the minute I saw her I was completely infatuated and dedicated to asking her out. Using my mother's idealism of patience being a virtue, I decided to start slowly by giving her daily compliments. She was at first understandably resistant to my pursuit of her, as I'm sure it probably appeared to border stalking. But what almost-thirty-year-old waitress would consider dating a seventeen-year-old flirtatious busboy? Though the odds were set against me, I was persistent.

To me she was the forbidden fruit, like the bowl of candy my mother placed in the middle of the coffee table, explaining that it was only for guests. I had picked my favorite candy from the bowl and was determined to get it unwrapped. Valentine's Day was approaching, so I checked the schedule to see that she was working that day. On the big day, I bought her a heart-shaped box of candy; she smiled as I presented it to her but seemed somewhat reluctant to take it.

The candy obviously wasn't going to be enough to win her over and I needed something much more substantial. I procured a can of white foam window cleaner from the storage area. I then used the cleaner to spray a heart with her name in it, on the front exterior window of the restaurant. This innovative move finally got her attention and convinced her to accept my invitation to go out with me. She may have agreed just to appease me, but I was fine with that. My thought was, you need to take your wins where you can get them. The date itself was less than impressive, though not uneventful.

Since I had spent all my money on the Camaro, I couldn't afford much, so I set up a table for two in one of the large back banquet rooms at the restaurant. I befriended the chef by offering him some baseball trading cards and had him make us a special meal. It was helpful that he had served her before, which meant that he already knew what she liked to eat. Unfortunately, since I was not old enough to drink, she was stuck with soda pop, but she didn't seem to mind. For dessert I scraped some remaining ice cream from the tubs in the back freezer, something I would often do before throwing away the containers.

After waiting patiently for her to finish her ice cream, I asked her if she wanted to see my new Camaro. I was thrilled when I heard from her the word "yes." She appeared excited after seeing the car, she loved the color and stated, "My favorite color is blue." Finding that she liked the car, I gathered up my confidence and asked if she wanted to go for a ride. Again, to my delight she agreed, and I thought, *Now I'm on a roll.* It was time for my big move: since she was going to be in the car, maybe I would have a chance to kiss her. Fearing she would change her mind; I ran to the passenger door to open it for her. She entered the car and said, "This is really nice." As we began our adventure, the sun was fading, and it was becoming dark outside.

While navigating the city streets, our conversation became a blur; I was too distracted admiring her lips as she talked, to comprehend anything she was saying. I was also still in shock that she was right there sitting next to me in my car. We stopped at a traffic light, and I thought this might be my only opportunity to steal my long-awaited kiss. I had to take the chance. I mustered up all the nerve I had left, puckered up my lips, aimed straight as I could, leaned over, and met her lips directly onto mine. It was awkward at first; she was mid-sentence, and I know it shocked her. I didn't expect it to go well, but then suddenly I felt her start to kiss me back. There was an immediate reaction somewhere below my belt line.

Not planning on being successful and thinking that I would never make it this far, I was now lost as to what my next move should be. Thankfully for me, she was more experienced than I was; she reached over and placed her hand on my tense virgin leg. I don't know how I was able to safely park the car, but somehow, I did. The next thing out of her mouth was, "How's the back seat?" I started to answer her as though it was a real question. Then as she climbed into the back, I came to the logical conclusion that her question was rhetorical.

It felt like an eternity for my shaking hands to fumble around and find the release button on my seatbelt. I was finally able to unlatch my belt and safely climb into the back seat to join her. Yes indeed, that was the first time I made love to a woman. Never in my wildest dreams did I think she would be receptive to my advances, but she was. Thanks to a beautiful blond waitress and a blue Camaro, this boy finally felt like he was a man.

Having absolutely no clue what I was doing, it was all over in a matter of minutes, but it was still one of the proudest moments of this young man's life. Rose asked that I not talk about our date while at work and that we not see each other again due to our age difference. It was very hard for me to hold my tongue around the other busboys and not brag about my conquest. Though I managed not to say anything, I had made a promise to her and wanted to oblige by her wishes.

Although I was able to refrain from talking about Rose, hiding the smile on my face when I saw her proved to be impossible. My mind would reminisce of our moment together every time she came into my view. It was now clear to me why songs were written about experiences like this. Once it happens, it's absorbed in your conscience like the ink from a tattoo on skin. Eventually my time with Rose at the restaurant came to an end, though the memory of our time together will always be with me.

VISITORS

My encounter with Rose helped to educate me on the importance of achieving privacy, and I made it a priority to try and establish my own residence. Now instead of saving to buy a car, I was saving to liberate myself from my parents' home. Although while putting money aside for my own place, I was distracted by my next big purchase. I ended up spending my savings on a new fad called the waterbed, which set me back a couple of years on my plan of moving out.

Thankfully I was rescued from my predicament when my parents told me of their own large purchase.

My parents sold their house in Oregon and had been renting one since we relocated to California. After renting for two years, they had set aside enough money for a down payment to buy another home. This meant I would finally be getting my own room, and I would no longer have to share one with my brother. The house they purchased was barely fourteen hundred square feet, but it had four bedrooms. The rooms in the house were small, though it didn't matter as I would now have a room to myself.

While moving into our new home, I received a call from my childhood friend Cary. I didn't think I would ever hear from him again, especially after the whole stolen bicycle incident. He stated that he was curious about California and wanted to see our new home. I was not against his visit, so I supplied him with our address. He made the trek down from Oregon in his dad's old green Toyota pickup. Knowing his father, I was surprised that he had allowed Cary to borrow the truck, and honestly didn't know if he had his dad's permission to use it.

Cary had brought a girl with him on his visit. During her introduction, he explained to me that they were just friends, while hinting that he wanted more from her. After their arrival, it quickly became apparent that this girl's intentions were to get closer to me than Cary. I made it clear to her that I was not interested, but it was too late as he had seen her attraction to me. I noticed that the circumstances had made him visibly upset, so we talked it out. Once I explained to him that I had no attraction toward the girl, we mended our friendship, and he returned to Oregon with her.

A few months later I received a phone call from the girl he had visited with. She had called to notify me of Cary's suicide. Upon his return his dad enrolled him in a rehabilitation center, where he used a bed sheet to hang himself. It was a very sad day; he had just turned eighteen. There was no note found, so it was unknown why he took his own life. I had some concerns over whether it had something to do with the girl or possibly issues with his father. Either way, I'm sure they were both feeling his loss and I had no prerogative to blame others for his passing. All I know is it was unnecessary and probably preventable.

At his funeral service, I spoke to his mother at length. In her voice I could hear the deep eternal sadness that had been forced upon her. I told her thank you for allowing him to be my friend. I guess trying to provide comfort is all we are left with when such a tragedy occurs. If I had a chance to talk to him again, I would tell him, "Wait just one more day, as tomorrow may be better." I realize this is all temporary, but I didn't understand the need for him to rush the situation. The conversation I had with his mom helped me to properly shoulder this weight. She made her view clear; that we cannot hold ourselves liable for the decisions and actions of others.

GOAL

It wasn't long after the funeral that I graduated high school and officially began my search for a full-time job, so I could finally get out on my own. The city just built the area's first indoor shopping mall, providing plenty of employment opportunities. I submitted several applications to stores at the mall before landing a position. The job I received was that of a shoe salesman at a popular athletic store. Selling shoes for a living, provided my older brother with plenty of sarcastic ammunition to launch my direction. His new nickname for me became "Mr. Bundy", referring to the character from the television show *Married with Children.*

My intent was to work at the shoe store only until I could establish myself in a more lucrative profession. I was in search of something that offered stability and financial security. This idealism was instituted in me by my father in his relentless hunt for a stable occupation. With a little research, I found that the careers offering the most stability were in government jobs. I originally had my sight set on becoming a real estate sales agent. But that choice did not offer long-term financial security. I set my real-estate dream aside, to fall in line with the rest of the working class. Looking back, I think this was the moment I stumbled into "the squirrel trap."

Routine government positions offering a consistent salary were the bait, like fresh strawberries set inside a trap. Once you tasted the benefits of going inside the trap, there was no way out. If you asked me today, I would say the decision to give up on my dream was a mistake. I now know that dreams should be pursued; the soul cannot be settled by seeking only comfort. Much of life is confronting our fears and anxieties that prevent us from taking necessary risks.

With my goal now set, I submitted applications to every local government agency I could find that didn't require a degree. These included the Department of Corrections, the Post Office, and the Sheriff's Department. While waiting for responses to my applications, I continued to work at the mall selling shoes. The one thing I couldn't help noticing was all the pretty girls employed at the mall. I made this observation during my daily hike to the food court for lunch. The route took me past the other shops, and I could see that many had female employees. I'm guessing for them this was a good place to work since they could go shopping whenever they wanted.

All these female workers were hard to ignore, but after my experiences with girls, I thought it was best to stay away from relationships for a while. My good intentions didn't last long, it turned out that my willpower was no match for one girl I spotted on my walk to lunch. It might have been advisable to have brought my lunch that day because once I saw her, I knew there was no going back. Alicia was her name, she worked at a small store that sold coffee mugs with pictures imprinted on them. She was yet another beautiful blond with an intoxicating smile.

On my way to the food court, I attempted to charmingly stroll past her small mug shop, trying my best not to gawk at her. Her effect on me caused me to feel as though I was drunk from my grandmother's wine. I began to lose my motor function and failed to avoid the large mall trashcan directly in my path. I walked straight into the trashcan that sat in front of her store. While recovering my broken ego from the mall floor, I saw that she had begun to smile at me. I couldn't have planned for a better ice breaker. I learned two things: she knew I was interested, and she had a good sense of humor.

After casually picking up the trashcan, I nonchalantly reached for one of the coffee mugs she was selling. There was no need for an introduction as we were both wearing name tags from the stores we worked at. Her job was to print the pictures on the coffee mugs, so I tried my best to appear interested in purchasing a mug. I ended up purchasing several mugs before returning to the shoe store only to realize I had forgotten to eat lunch. Of course, I had asked Alicia to go out with me and she agreed, which made it worth all the mugs I just purchased. For Christmas that year, my whole family received coffee mugs with my picture on them.

We went on several dates, and I took her to her senior prom. She liked that I was an older man, even if I was still technically a teenager and only one year older. I was again smitten, and after almost a year together, I thought that if this is the one, I'd better move quickly before I lose her too. At the age of nineteen I was finally able to move out of my parents' house. Alicia and I moved into a small apartment together, and I proudly made her my fiancée.

My belief that we would spend the rest of our lives together was spoiled by her mother's purposeful interruption. Her mother was extremely overbearing, upon meeting her I could tell she didn't care for me much. Employed as a waitress at a local restaurant, she always wanted a better life for herself and her daughter. She was not happy that I was just a shoe salesman and that I did not come from a rich family. Willing to do whatever it took to see that her daughter married someone of wealth, her influence became impossible to repel.

My efforts to thwart her mother's unimaginable schemes to tear Alicia and I apart were unsuccessful. In the end her mother was the true reason we never got married, but I blamed our breakup on myself. I felt my dedication to achieving more financial success eventually pushed Alicia away. I thought by working many hours of overtime I might receive a promotion to a manager position, thereby proving my self-worth to her mom. I had spent too much precious time attempting to validate myself to someone that didn't matter and trying to fix something that was never broken. She just may have been my one true love—my soulmate, as they say, but now she is just the one that got away.

MILITARY

Losing Alicia took a toll on my emotional well-being and caused me to turn my full attention to my career search. I was contacted by a few government agencies in reference to my employment applications. One of the agencies interested in hiring me was the Los

Angeles County Sheriff's Department. I jumped at the opportunity to test for the position. The deputy testing process proved to be very long and arduous and did not result in my appointment to an academy. I was told that I performed well on the exams, but that I did not have enough experience. The background investigator processing my application suggested that it might serve me well to gain some exposure to military training, before reapplying.

During the sheriff testing process, I continued to work as a shoe salesman at the mall. Alicia's coffee mug shop had closed, I was alone and doing my best to avoid relationships. Though my weakness for girls once again caused me to succumb to the power of attraction. Tina, like Alicia, was of course another blond. We met at a local foosball tournament where she was my opponent. Tina had added pink highlights to her hair, which I found attractive; I thought it showed she cared about her looks. I was caught up in her façade and ignoring the fact that bright colors in the wild, were there to act as a warning as well as an attraction.

Tina and I seemed to be a good fit as we both had the same interests. With my relationship track record so far, I figured I again needed to either jump in with both feet or run. I jumped in and asked her to marry me. In this situation, though, I may have moved too quickly. Our marriage was one of convenience, which made trust and commitment questionable, particularly for her. She was aware that I wanted to become a deputy and understood my need to join the military to make that happen. She was not a fan of my plan but accepted my decision. Explaining my intentions to my mother did not go as smoothly as I had hoped either. My parents did not approve of the military, and my mother wanted me to follow my ambitions of working in real estate.

In my research, I found that of all the military branches, the Army offered the most attractive selection of training courses. I located an Army recruiting office and enlisted. Signing the military recruitment documents and going over what was expected of me during training was stressful. With the knowledge that basic training would be physically and mentally challenging, I started exercising daily and studying military rankings. The day of my departure to basic, I was picked up by my recruiter and driven to a processing center in Los Angeles. After an overnight stay at the center, I was deposited on a plane with several other recruits and flown to the Fort Leonard Wood Army Base in Missouri. I was very nervous about my new adventure but because of my preparation I was confident in my potential for success.

My initial interaction with the personnel at the Army base reception center was very strenuous. I knew it was designed to be that way, but knowing this did not ease my tension. I thought the humiliation of having my head shaved would be the worst part, though as it turned out I was wrong. After being yelled at for several hours and having all the hair on my head removed, it was inoculation time.

Receiving the shots was traumatizing, to say the least; the vaccination delivery method was anything but gentle. The enlisted military medical personnel performing the injections were not concerned about your comfort. There was no empathy involved in distributing the shots, as they had had to endure the same process. The ice-cold penicillin shot in my buttocks literally caused me to drag my right leg around for a full day. My only relief came from the knowledge that I was not alone in this torment.

SERVICE

Encountering my fellow recruits made for an enlightening experience. They arrived from different states all around the country, and most possessed accents in their speech. The accents made some of the recruits difficult for me to understand. I felt completely displaced. It was unsettling, but I didn't feel alone because I could see the other recruits felt similarly. We were all undergoing the same process and dealing with the pressure of performing in an unknown environment.

Basic training was full of purpose but also strenuous, exhausting, and at times dangerous. The occurrence of injuries was not uncommon, though safety was always a priority for the staff. There were sprained ankles, broken bones, and an occasional powder burn from the firing of a weapon. The recruits were provided with standard safety gear and given instructions on its proper use. Remaining alert during these demonstrations was essential to avoid injury. This was particularly true for the new recruits since none of them had ever previously operated an assault rifle or a grenade launcher.

Witnessing one of my fellow recruits injured during a training event showed me the importance of always being alert. The training involved the testing of nerve agent protective gear. The platoon marched into a small structure where the testing was to occur. After entering the building, we were required to remove our gas mask, so that we may experience the effect of the gas without the protective gear. The intent of the training was to demonstrate how our protective gear could prevent the gas from penetrating. The effects of the gas, without the mask, were blurred vision and temporary loss of respiration.

Exiting the building involved navigating a short set of stairs. The recruit directly in front of me failed to grasp the handrail while making his departure and slipped on one of the steps. He then fell striking his mouth on the handrail. The impact with the metal handrail knocked out several of his front teeth and he was sent immediately for medical attention. Although gruesome, accidents like this were expected when instructions were not followed.

Our training was extended from the normal eight weeks to ten. Along with the added time, my platoon's curriculum was expanded to include several different types of weapons. I was a little curious as to why we were being trained in such weapons. I didn't see the need for extra training as my military operations specialty was just that of a flight medic. The platoon's first real command from our captain, ordering us to board a military transport plane, helped to answer this question. After boarding the plane, our lieutenant advised us that we were being dispatched to a foreign country that was currently at war. I thought at first this may be another exercise—that is until my staff sergeant handed me a loaded magazine for my M16 rifle.

In our training we learned that the average survival time for a soldier after landing in a war zone wasn't long. Because of this I tried to mentally prepare myself for what could possibly be my last day on earth. There was no typical chatter from the other recruits; in fact, there was not a word being said. I could only hear the plane's roaring engines, and all I could focus on was the frightened stares now pinned on the faces of my battle buddies. I am sure many of their thoughts were about loved ones they might not ever see again.

After several hours of sitting on the runway, the plane's engines shut down, its doors opened, and we were told to deboard. The trip had been canceled, and since my rank was only that of a specialist, I was not informed of why. Due to this event, at the end of my service, I was granted a war ribbon and the right to a veteran's status. Though since I believed this was done by mistake, I have never used this privilege; I didn't feel I earned it with my only contribution being sitting on a runway. My Army contract was just for three years, but I never regretted a minute of it. During that time, I met a group of strangers who somehow developed a camaraderie so effective that they were willing to trust each other with their own lives.

The ability to trust others is something, I believe, they brought with them when they enlisted. This was best demonstrated to me on our final run together. Upon graduation each platoon is given the chance to develop its own mascot to where on a T-shirt during the final colors run. Since we were trained as medics, my platoon developed the character of an older male doctor wearing his work attire, and a stethoscope around his neck. We decided to use our sergeant's last name and went with the first name Papa.

After dawning our new outfits and proceeding to the run site, we were promptly stopped and scolded by the sergeant. He made it clear that he did not appreciate our new fashion statement. He said that the picture of an old man displayed across our chest, with the words Papa Woody 4th Platoon was "inappropriate attire." Though it was well known that he was not favored by the troops. In fact, it was rumored that at one point one of his troops had switched his baby powder with cleaning detergent. An experience, I'm sure, that could not have been too comfortable on his privates.

Our reward for our misdeeds that day was being the only platoon to run with our T-shirts turned inside out. Not knowing how our new motto would be received, each platoon member fully understood the possible consequences of our actions. Though we were each willing to accept the risk. We agreed to either be triumphant or fail as a team and share in any necessary repercussions.

Although not the best analogy, this rare type of human dedication to others is not to be taken for granted. Many soldiers have fought and risked their lives for others, earning the right to be called a veteran. They have trusted us that their sacrifices would not be in vain. Now after serving, when I see war veterans, I am honored by their presents more so than that of a celebrity. Their service goes mostly unappreciated when it really deserves to be celebrated. Our lives would not be the same without veterans; their sacrifice is the reason freedom exists, and why I am allowed to write this story.

CHAPTER FIVE

Ages 25 to 30

A chieving my goal of completing Army basic training, and eventually an honorable discharge, was only
made possible with the relief offered by letters from my
mother. Stuck in an Army barrack far away from family, her reassur-
ing words offered me hope. For most recruits, inspirational letters
from family members provided them with the necessary motivation
needed to continue. Her letters helped to occupy my mind, while
allowing me to stay abreast of the developments back home.

My marriage, on the other hand, did not fare as well while I was
away. Our relationship was already strained, and my new bride was
not very patient with me, being gone for so long. After I completed
basic training, she advised me that she was pregnant. She decided it
was bad timing to have a child since I would not be there to assist her,
and it would be best to terminate the pregnancy. I did not agree with
her decision and attempted to talk her out of it. I grappled with ideas
of how to prevent her from having an abortion, while still trying to be
supportive of her needs.

She went through with the termination, and it was almost ten years later before I found out her real motivation. During an argument, she confessed that her pregnancy was not due to intercourse with me. Her insistence on the termination now made more sense. At first when she told me, I felt stupid, thinking I should have known. I chose not to listen to my intuition and instead decided to rely on trust. I found myself reviewing all the time that we had wasted and wishing that she had revealed this information to me many years earlier. Though I could only speculate on how difficult it must have been for her to maintain this secret for so long. Her eventual divulgence of this information put an end to our marriage. This was a difficult life lesson to learn about trusting others and ignoring my own gut feelings.

Several months after returning home from the Army, I could tell things had changed. I didn't understand why at the time, as I didn't yet know about her affair. I just knew the affection we once felt for each other was all but gone. I chose to blame the cause of this on the abortion and my time away. We mistakenly decided to ignore the issue, and instead of focusing on the relationship, our attention turned to our individual careers. I resubmitted my application to the Sheriff's Department immediately upon my return. This time my testing ended with better results. I made it through all the interviews and exams to receive an invitation to an academy. The next academy was almost a year off, so I took a job in construction while preparing myself.

Tina had been living in a small apartment while I was away, so we decided it was time for us to purchase our first home. Tina also expressed to me that since things were becoming more stable, she would like to try again to have a child together. Thinking the first pregnancy was mine, I was surprised that she wanted to try again, but I was glad to know that she still desired children. When I informed her of all that was transpiring, my mother was happy to hear that she would soon have a grandchild. Although she was still not elated about my career choice.

After moving into our new home, Tina had our first and only child together. We had a boy and decided to name him Cameron. My mother was hoping for a granddaughter, as she already had three boys of her own, but I was happy with a son. My mother now has four grandsons and no granddaughters. Life is that way sometimes; we are provided with wonderful gifts, though not always packaged the way we expected.

The deputy sheriff academy approached quickly, and before I knew it, I was in. Buying a home, having a child, and starting a new career all at once may not have been the best approach to life. With the homework, uniform preparation, and a newborn child I began to doubt my ability to complete the academy. The traffic-riddled two-hour drive each way every day also did not help the situation. Though feeling young and invincible, I wasn't considering the consequences. I took comfort in the fact that this, like life, was only temporary. To keep my spirits up, I also attempted to seek out humor wherever possible. I often found this making light of my drill instructors' mishaps such as with Deputy Chris.

Running and exercise drills were part of the daily routine in this academy. The training did not take place in a rural setting as with the Army, but on the populated public streets in the city of Los Angeles. For one of our drill instructors, the task of running on the street proved to be too much. Chris was a rookie instructor; he was tall with blond hair and resembled the actor Dolph Lundgren from the *Rocky* movie series. It was evident that he enjoyed demonstrating his masculinity in his attempts to impress the senior drill instructors. His specialty was berating the recruits for their inability to run in formation the entire time we were running. His dedication to belittling the recruits on the platoon runs was relentless. Unfortunately for Chris, he was not a good multitasker. He was unable to run, yell, and pay attention at the same time.

One day while running alongside the platoon and yelling out instructions, he failed to notice a stop sign directly in front of him. He was suddenly surprised when he ran full stride straight into the sign, knocking him to the ground. The stop sign did its job and stopped him in his tracks. Still dazed by the impact, though wanting to reaffirm his authority, Chris immediately jumped to his feet and continued his yelling charade.

The stop sign had left quite an impression on him; there was now a long indentation and a red mark running from his forehead to his chin. His newly acquired, clearly visible blemish had spoiled his aesthetically perfect face. His appearance, accompanied by his attempt to disregard the collision, made it impossible for the recruits to keep their composure. The inability for the recruits to retain their laughter infuriated him, so he added another two miles to our run that day. If you asked the recruits, they would say the extra miles were well worth the entertainment he provided us with. In fact, we nicknamed the stop sign "Pride" in his honor.

MARRIAGE

My reward for the successful completion of the sheriff academy was an assigned position at a custody facility, meaning a jail. The facility was located not far from my residence, and the shorter commute was a welcome adjustment. Performing the required duties of my new profession inside of this jail was not the same as I assumed it would be. I discovered that the training I received had not fully prepared me for the impact of this environment. It would have been helpful had they provided us with some acting classes. Entering the complex, it became apparent it would be necessary for me to portray a different image of myself. In here it was beneficial to play the part of someone tougher than I was, like an actor or a politician would. I knew that displaying weakness could possibly cost you your life, so I relied once again on the demonstrations of strength shown by my father.

Eventually I concluded that if I retained self-dignity and continual respect for others, working here would be safe. Gaining inmates' respect was achieved by providing the same in return, while maintaining a command presence. Like my fellow military recruits, these male inmates all came from different backgrounds and had different stories. I didn't know anything about their individual circumstances, I only knew of the reason they were institutionalized.

Characteristic of my father, they were not going to share much about who they were, because that would require the conveying of their feelings. I knew they were each individual and, like this book, they could not be judged by their cover. In my association with them I applied the wisdom a teacher once disbursed to me. She stated that we are all mentally one-year-olds in any given subject until we learn it, and then we mature and grow. Studying from the academy books was one thing, but growing and gaining knowledge of inmates required observing human interaction.

My observations showed me that humans, in a manner similar to animals, seem to instinctually test weakness in others. No different from children testing their parents' resolve, inmates would also constantly test my self-respect. Their efforts included the use of intimidation as a tool to try and force me to cave to their requests. I have often witnessed this ritual in politicians and now saw it occurring with the inmates. Not allowing my emotions to overcome me, enabled me to remain calm and avoid reacting to the pressure. To do this, I would occasionally need to apply a method my mother often used.

She would count to ten before reacting. The use of this technique supplied me with the time needed to develop a proper response, to an inmate's request.

This environment, in a way, prepared me for my role as a husband and a parent. During spousal disagreements, I applied my jail-learned methods of portraying strength without displaying aggression. This technique seemed to be effective in dispensing my fatherly duties but did not fare as well with my spouse. My home life proved to be, at times, more difficult than my chosen career. I was assigned to the night shift and was required to work many mandatory overtime hours. The job stole from me the opportunity to spend essential quality time with Tina and Cameron. This is when I saw just how the "trap" works: It steals from you the most precious gift you have to offer, your time.

My time away from home had a similar effect on my relationship with Tina as my military career. The new gift of parenthood came with more responsibility, stress, and financial burdens. Still Cameron, or as we call him, Cam, added a new element of joy to our lives. My son is nothing less than a gift to me, and I cherished every moment of his childhood. The arrival of our son and concentrating on his needs had temporarily relieved some of the tension that had developed between us, but unfortunately it didn't last long.

Taking care of Cam and working a full-time job placed a lot of stress on Tina. She became overwhelmed and began to have emotional breakdowns. Some days she would lock herself in the bathroom and cry for hours. We turned to my mother, asking her for help caring for Cam while I was at work. I believe her assistance was the only reason Tina was able to work through her mental health issues. Having to rely on my mother for help was not the ideal situation, but it made me appreciate her presence. I now have a lot more sympathy for single parents and those who have no relatives to rely on.

Due to her extreme emotional outbreaks, Tina and I made the decision to seek the help of a professional. We obtained a referral to a doctor who could prescribe her medication. At first the medication did not help; it only made things worse to the point where she became violent. Injuries I suffered from her anger included stitches from a blow to the head by a chair and on my elbow from a thrown drinking glass I blocked. Her violent outburst forced me to temporarily relocate my son to my mom's, for his safety. Even with my injuries, I was not willing to abandon her; I believed it was not her fault and she just needed help. Staying with her was my decision, and I wouldn't advise anyone else to risk their personal safety by doing this.

Thankfully, within a few months, we were able to find a prescription that finally relieved her symptoms. It was comforting to have her back to normal and to trust her with Cam again. I was present during the time she met with the psychiatrist; she brought forward information previously unknown to me about her suffering abuse as a child. The psychiatrist led us to believe that this childhood trauma had something to do with her ongoing emotional issues. Although I was sympathetic, since I had a good childhood, it was difficult for me to empathize with how this affected her. Because of this, when Cam was old enough to date, I advised him if he was serious about the girl, he should find out as much as he could about her childhood.

With the doctor's diagnosis, I excused her actions as a learned emotional defense response. I guess her stress caused her to act in an aggressive manner, just as she had as a child for protection—although she had no valid reason to make me her target. Since it was not my burden it was difficult for me to bear without becoming defensive. I felt I didn't deserve to be the object of her violence. Accepting the doctor's explanation was the only way I could justify her actions in my attempt to move past this.

PATROL

My time spent working in jail facilities showed me that incarceration did not improve inmates' lives. Jail temporarily prevented them from committing more crimes by keeping them out of public and away from citizens. Though being confined with other hardened criminals did not provide a balanced enough environment for their successful reintegration. Witnessing this solidified my decision not to have Tina arrested for her actions against me. I may have unwittingly prevented her from dealing with the repercussions of her violence. But I felt that having her freedom taken away would make it difficult for her to recover and preserve a place for her in Cam's life.

The original intent of incarceration was to keep people with bad intentions from harming public citizens. This purpose has since been mutated by politicians into a revenue-creating machine. Caught up in the system, those not having the financial means to purchase their freedom, are plucked off the vine like low-hanging fruit. Without separating the justified from the unjustified, upon arrest the less fortunate have their rights stripped and their property confiscated. This process can serve as an inspiration to worsen the intent of those jailed for minor offenses. Their lives become impacted by negative reporting placed on their records, reducing their employment value. Left without the funds to properly support their family, they have little choice but to look to crime or the government for support and survival.

Programs designed by bureaucrats to help rehabilitate inmates, were based on the ability to create, transfer, and expend funds. Inmate integration into these programs created a level of confusion, which made it difficult to determine the difference between criminals. The original idea may have been to assist inmates, but corruption has long since destroyed any successful program progress. From what I have seen, these programs now mainly serve to funnel government assets into the hands of politically friendly contractors. I believe this process will persist, since the public continues to allow their tax revenue to be stolen through political manipulation of the system.

My experience has shown me that with all the incompetent influence, custody facilities now serve as a tool for circulating funds through branches of government and corporations. I fear this problem can only be fixed through divine intervention, and I am glad I was never fully mentally indoctrinated into their servitude. Though, Sadly, in this modern world, jails and laws remain necessary. Laws as a functioning deterrent and jails as the only way to humanely separate the truly wicked and protect the innocent.

Removing myself from my soap box, that I feel I earned. I will say that my attempt to remain open-minded while dealing with inmates made custody a successful working environment for me. Besides responding to a few fights, I spent much of my time watching cameras and opening doors. The worst part was the several important family events I missed; time I know I can't get back. Although sacrificing time for money was a necessity, in hindsight it was seldom worth it.

The family trip I regretted missing the most was a vacation in Hawaii. After spending several years working in custody facilities, I earned the opportunity to attend patrol training. Unfortunately, the patrol academy was scheduled to begin on the same date as the trip. I made the training my priority, though if I had the opportunity to go back and accompany my family on the trip instead, I certainly would. I didn't know it at the time, but it would be the last chance for me to vacation with my father.

While at the patrol academy, I was not thinking of my family in Hawaii. I was strictly concentrating on learning everything I could about life as a street cop. To prepare us for our new working environment, patrol academy instructors shared many precautionary tales and the worst possible scenarios. We trained extensively in the use of weapons and emergency vehicles, practicing our response to different situations. The training lasted two weeks, the same amount of time that my parents and brothers spent in Hawaii.

As with my custody assignment, the reality of patrol was very different from what I perceived it to be. Upon completion of my training, my first post was at a station in a city thirty minutes north of Los Angeles. I was assigned to work in a crime car on the night shift, as most new recruits were. On my first shift, I showed up in my pressed class-A uniform, wearing my shiny new badge and highly polished boots. I was to meet up with my training officer, Ryan. Training officers were referred to as the "T.O.," but I liked to refer to Ryan as "my partner," and you will soon know why.

Ryan was a large man standing over six feet tall, with a serious disposition. He had over sixteen years' experience as a deputy; he was a seasoned professional who did not appreciate trainee mistakes. The first few weeks amounted to long nights of writing reports, issuing citations, and booking suspects. Many of our calls involved petty theft and domestic disputes.

Thankfully, I only had to draw my duty weapon once during this time. We were dispatched to assist in a burglary call and arrived at the back of the reported location. While watching the rear of the residence, I observed the figure of a young man run out of the back door. The suspect was wearing a backpack and met the description in the call. I looked over at Ryan and told him I was going in foot pursuit of the suspect. He nodded with approval, so I leaped out of the patrol vehicle and began to run after the suspect.

In his attempt to escape, the young man scaled an eight-foot block wall. Since I was fresh out of the academy I was in good physical shape, and able to follow him over the wall. Landing on the opposite side, I saw that I was now in someone's backyard. It had become dark outside, but I was still able to make out the suspect's silhouette as he ran. I continued to chase after him as he darted to the opposite side of the yard. The darkness helped to conceal his path, causing me to temporarily lose sight of him.

No longer having him in sight and not knowing if he was armed, I drew my duty weapon. I noticed a small kiddie style swimming pool lying in the yard and thought he might have crawled under it to hide. While pointing my gun at the pool, I used my foot to flip it over, hoping I would not be presented with the barrel of a gun. As I was flipping over the small pool, I heard a large bang sound in the direction I had just come from. It was Ryan; he was not as in shape and fresh from an academy as I was, and it had taken him a little more effort to get over the block wall.

Turning my attention back to the pool, I saw that the suspect was not there, which was honestly a relief. I then noticed a figure to my right, that was crouched down in the corner of the yard. I shined my flashlight and pointed my gun in that direction. As the suspect's figure became illuminated by my light, he jumped up and began to run toward me. Having made his way over the wall and seeing that the suspect was going to attack me, Ryan began to run full speed toward him. Ryan slammed into the suspect like a freight train, the impact lifted him off his feet and straight into the air. Ryan landed right on top of him, squashing him into the ground.

Since I no longer needed my duty weapon, I holstered it and fitted the suspect with my new handcuffs. Upon searching the suspect, I found no weapon, only burglary tools in his backpack. While Ryan was standing up and brushing the dirt off his uniform, I noticed some blood coming from his forehead. When I inquired about it, he replied, "I'm fine, it came from the block wall I had to climb over." After a short chuckle to his reply about his injury from the wall, I had the homeowner identify the suspect as the man who attempted to burglarize her home.

Having Ryan as my partner that night was fortunate. Come to find out, the suspect was only fifteen years old, and I couldn't imagine the outcome if he had had a gun. Not long after the young man's arrest, Ryan and I were assigned a new patrol area on the outlying edge of the city. This area was known for its high crime and use of illegal methamphetamine drugs. While working in the area, we issued many traffic citations and conducted several arrests. But none of this would prepare me for what I would encounter next in my career as a deputy.

SHOOTING

My night shift began like any other: I arrived at the station early, collected all the gear, and loaded it into the patrol vehicle. Ryan arrived shortly after wearing a rare smile on his face, revealing that he was in a good mood. He was pleased with the gear after inspecting my preparation work and climbed into the driver's seat. The commute from the station to our assigned patrol area was about thirty minutes. Our route took us by an old Mexican restaurant, where Ryan decided to stop to grab some burritos. This was an unexpected treat and a break in our routine, most nights we did not have time to eat.

As in some bad movie plot, just as we started to enjoy our burritos, we heard an emergency broadcast over the police radio. The call was a dispatch for our unit, concerning a burglary in progress in our area. Ryan looked at his burrito, let out a long sigh, and threw it into the trash. He then turned to me and said, "Come on, let's go." We jumped into the patrol car, put on the emergency lights, and sped away into the night, toward the location of the call.

While he was driving, I was reviewing the incoming dispatch information, to ascertain the exact location of the residence and the suspect's description. Having no electronic navigation systems at the time and sitting in the passenger seat, the job of navigator was left to me. This was a very financially distressed area that lacked proper streetlights, making it difficult to see through the darkness. To complicate the situation, many of the street signs were removed by vandals. Still, somehow, I was able to direct us to the proper location.

We turned down the street toward the address provided in the call, and I was able to identify a large muscular man fitting the suspect's description. When he came into view, I saw that he was departing from the residence indicated in the call. Upon noticing us, he turned away and began to walk at a fast pace in the opposite direction. Watching him walk away from us, I saw that his movements were stiff, and his body was very rigid. As we made our approach, the suspect clenched his hands into fists and appeared to be very upset. Ryan stopped the patrol vehicle in the middle of the street. We both exited the vehicle, while withdrawing our duty weapons from our holsters. I then called out to the suspect, announcing us as deputies and ordering him to stop.

Hearing my voice, he stopped, turned, and in a stiff robot-like motion, began to walk rapidly toward Ryan. Ryan, not knowing if the man was armed, aimed his pistol at him. The suspect reached

Ryan in seconds, lurched forward with his hands extended, and grabbed the barrel of Ryans gun. Without hesitation Ryan pulled the guns trigger, the fired bullet entered the suspect's abdomen, causing him to release the barrel. At this point it was obvious the suspect was under the influence of some type of narcotics. He was bleeding profusely from the gunshot and did not seem at all fazed by his critical injury. It was a terrible turn of events, and far from being over.

Ryan backed away from the suspect and transmitted an assistance call over his hand-held radio. The suspect's attention had turned away from Ryan; his focus was now on the open driver's door of our patrol vehicle. He made it to the vehicle and began to reach inside toward the unit's shotgun. I knew the shotgun was loaded and allowing him to retrieve it might have deadly consequences for Ryan and me. I pointed my Beretta 9mm sidearm at him and carefully lined up my sights in the middle of his chest. As he grasped onto the shotgun and started to pull, I placed my index finger on the trigger of my duty weapon and began to squeeze. If he successfully retrieved the weapon from the vehicle, I would be forced to pull the trigger and possibly end his life. I was completely aware that the repercussions of not pulling the trigger could mean the end of mine.

Thankfully, he was unable to manipulate the release mechanism and retrieve the shotgun. The weapon remained locked securely in place, removing the need for me to discharge my Beretta. After discovering he could not access the shotgun, the suspect exited the vehicle. His clothes now soaked with blood from his injury, he started walking toward a residential driveway, adjacent to the patrol vehicle. He entered the driveway, where Ryan met up with him and attempted to detain him. The suspect resisted, resulting in a brief fist fight between him and Ryan. Seeing that I was running over to assist, the suspect turned his focus toward me. He turned and was now swinging his fist in my direction.

His right fist made contact and struck me on the left side of my head. Before I was able to shake off the effects of his punch, I felt him grab onto the grip of my now holstered duty weapon. My trained instinctual response was to quickly place my right hand over the top of my gun's holster strap. I then wedged my hand down between the strap and my belt, which prevented the weapon from being removed. I bent at the knees and transferred my body weight onto the strap, enabling me to further secure my gun in its holster.

With his hands now around my gun's grip, the suspect began to pull upward, attempting to remove it from my holster. Exerting some type of superhuman strength, he lifted my entire body off the ground. I could literally hear my leather belt begin to tear as he yanked at the grip of the gun. He was now so close to me I felt a flash of hot air on my face, as he exhaled the contents of his lungs. The drug-filled stench of his breath supplied me with a rush of adrenalin that ran through my body. I was no longer trying to detain the suspect; I was now in a desperate fight for my life. My body had entered fight or flight mode, and being under his control, flight was not an option.

With my only free hand, I tried to fight back, but he was twice my size and not feeling any pain. I was physically outmatched, with death literally staring me in the face. It was like dancing with the devil, and it was not some romantic movie; there was no pale moonlight, only faded streetlamps. In my peripheral view I could see a streetlight illuminate Ryan's figure. Ryan recognized that the suspect was trying to disarm me, and that this was a life-or-death situation. I heard Ryan's gun discharge as he fired several rounds at the suspect, attempting to make him let go of my gun. I could feel the impact of each bullet as it struck the suspect's body. I heard several rounds shot, before the suspect's hands released the grip of my gun, as he fell lifeless to the ground.

Once the suspect released me, I looked up to see several other deputies running in our direction. The arriving deputies quickly secured the scene and checked on the suspect. I noticed the last shot had blown my right hand clean off my holster. Lifting my hand, I saw that my ring finger had been partially removed from one of the bullets Ryan had fired. The pain did not affect me until after I saw the blood coming from my now-distorted hand. When I saw this, I felt an instant incredible stinging sensation, like I had just been stung by a hundred bees in the same spot.

The wound to my hand raised my concern that I may have been struck by another bullet and had not yet realized it. This frightening thought caused my toes to curl up inside my boots, that were now soaked with the suspect's blood. I used my left hand and, with the help of other deputies, frantically searched my midsection for more injuries. Finding no other bullet holes was a major relief, as the one that struck my hand was only inches from my liver. Having found I had no other bodily injuries; I made my way across the street to an arriving ambulance.

A paramedic grasped my arm and raised my hand above my head. He then guided me into the ambulance, where he wrapped up my hand and the remnants of my finger. Sitting in the ambulance I could see safety personnel start to flood the small rural street. Watching the suspect's body being loaded into another ambulance gave me a sense of relief, and a simultaneous feeling of sadness. The danger was over, but a man had just lost his life.

RECOVERY

The emergency personnel provided me with a morphine injection for the pain. This medication provided me with an instant welcome relief from the throbbing in my hand. I was transported to the hospital and treated by the emergency room physician; due to the extent of the damage, he had a difficult time deciding whether he should amputate my finger. After examining my hand, the doctor said, "We need to remove that damaged finger." Ryan had called the emergency room phone to check on me and overheard the doctor's statement. In a conversation with the doctor, Ryan was able to talk him into trying to save it, explaining to him that it was my gun hand.

As Ryan and the doctor were on the phone discussing the verdict on my finger, I felt the morphine start to work making me delirious; I was not used to the strength of this medication. When the doctor held the phone to my ear so that Ryan could talk to me, I asked him for a glass of water. Both he and the doctor found my request humorous, and they started to laugh. I was confused at their laughter; I only knew that I was thirsty. Ryan replied, "Sure, partner, I'll get you some water, and I'm going to have that doctor save that finger." Because of the ensuing investigation, that was the last conversation I had with my partner, Ryan.

In the emergency room, the nurses cut off the rest of my uniform, as it was covered in blood and had to be preserved by detectives for evidence. I was then transferred to a room for an overnight stay and scheduled to have surgery the next day. The following day they operated on my hand; the procedure took almost five hours to complete. When the bullet struck the bone in my hand, it splintered, and the surgeon had to remove all the metal fragments.

During the surgery the doctor inserted two metal rods in my finger, securing it to my hand. I remained in the hospital for several days. Apparently, they needed to conduct more X-rays of my hand and my head where I was hit by the suspect's fist. The X-rays didn't indicate any injuries to my head. Finding this out, my mother, always by my side and trying to lift my spirits, made the statement, "I told you there was nothing up there." Once I was stable, they released me from the hospital.

Attempting to restore the use of my hand so that I could return to work, I incurred three more surgeries in the following year. The recovery and physical therapy process was agonizing, to say the least. The worst part was having to re-learn performing simple tasks like tying my shoes and signing my name. After each surgery I was instructed to keep my hand elevated to repel the pain. This forced me to rest my arm on the middle console of my truck while driving. With my finger pinned and wrapped up, it gave the constant uncomfortable impression that I was flipping off the other drivers. I was the recipient of some disgruntled remarks. This new predicament forced me to gain an appreciation, for the plight of those with unsettling physical deformities.

Along with the physical issues I suffered from the shooting, I also endured many hours of psychological therapy. The post-traumatic stress disorder (PTSD) was almost intolerable. This issue never really goes away, regardless of how much therapy you receive. It causes sleepless nights that dissipate over time, but recalling the incident can still cause anxiety. Memories of the incident can trigger a slow-motion projection reel to roll in my mind. It's like a broken record that you can't shut off, constantly skipping over the same annoying song.

After a year of surgeries, physical therapy, and testing on my hand, they considered my injury permanent. Since I was unable to recoup the full use of my hand, I was declared unfit for duty. The department ordered me to turn over my badge and uniforms. I would now no longer have the right to wear the color of authority I had earned. An investigation took place, and the department determined that I was to receive a mandatory retirement due to my service-related injury. This news was difficult for me to accept; I was not prepared to have my career end just as it was beginning.

The family of the deceased suspect had filed a lawsuit against the county. With the pending lawsuit and the fact that I was shot by my partner, they wanted the incident swept under the rug. For this reason, the department would not issue me the normal commendation or retirement ceremony. I was now also not allowed to talk to my partner, so the next time I saw him was at trial. I was required to testify in the lawsuit, which was not very helpful to my PTSD. The only way I felt safe entering the courthouse was while wearing my bulletproof vest. I was told that my testimony ensured I would be released from any liability. The lawsuit was eventually settled by the department. Only seven years in, at the age of thirty-five, my career as a deputy was over.

All of this proved to be too much pressure on my marriage. The ensuing arguments included Tina's admittance to her previous lie about aborting my child. Upon hearing this, I knew there would be no reconciliation. I had lost not only my career but now my marriage too. This domino of occurrences took a toll on my young son, Cam. Since I was now not working, I started to spend as much time as I could with him. I tried to constantly assure him things would be okay, even if I didn't completely believe it myself.

FATHER

Cam was now just eight years old, and spending time with him every day provided the perfect break from dealing with my divorce. Tina and I agreed on a living and custody arrangement that best fit Cam's needs. Just as I thought the worst was behind me, I received a phone call from my mother. She informed me that my father had been taken to the hospital because of an infection in his gall bladder. After speaking with her, I conducted a little research and found that this was a common issue, which helped to set my mind at ease.

Thankfully, my father had not yet been told of my pending divorce. I was glad to know that this information would not be in his thoughts. In his condition he didn't need the extra stress. Once he was admitted, I went to visit him. Seeing that he was very lethargic and knowing I still needed to pick up Cam, I didn't stay long. Before leaving, I explained to him that I had to go and get Cam from school, but that my mother was on her way. As I raised myself up from the chair, I noticed that his feet were uncovered. I located his socks, placed them on his feet and said goodbye. My father looked at me and stated, "Thanks. Love you, kiddo. Go take care of my grandson."

After picking up Cam from school, I took him to our favorite local miniature golf course. It was a special place that we had first visited with his grandfather months before. I thought we could spend some time there until his mom was off work and could watch him. I wanted to go back and see my father and wasn't ready to expose Cam to that type of environment. While walking a few yards behind me on the course, Cam stopped and called out to me, saying, "Dad, don't leave me." Concerned, I turned to look at him. As he came into view, I could clearly see the image of my father standing next to him.

The jarring sound of my ringing mobile phone dragged my consciousness back into reality. Answering the phone, I heard the voice of my aunt, telling me that there was something wrong with my father, and that I needed to get to the hospital. When I looked up after the call, I could only see Cam; the figure of my father was gone. I knew then, without anyone telling me, I just had my last visit with him. I walked over to Cam and told him that it was time for us to leave. With a golf ball–sized lump in my throat and trying my best to restrain my emotions. I explained to Cam that Grandpa wasn't feeling well, and he would need to stay with his mother for the night.

On the way to drop off Cam, thoughts of him and my father together began to race through my mind. I recalled a time when he couldn't even pronounce the word "Grandpa," and instead what often came out was "Crappa." Hearing this my father would laugh finding the mispronunciation humorous. He enjoyed having grand-kids and was proud to be a grandfather. I was sad, but thanks to my son's comforting presents, I was not upset. Cam's calm demeanor, gained from his ignorance, brought me a sense of peace. The inno-cence of children can certainly brighten even our worst days.

The commute to the hospital would take at least one hour and I was not in the right mental state to operate a vehicle. Thankfully, I had a deputy friend whom I used to work with, that lived nearby and was willing to give me a ride. I arrived at the hospital and pro-ceeded straight to the room where I had last seen my father. The room was now filled with my entire family, including my mother, brothers, aunts, and uncle. I walked over to my father's bedside where I observed his lifeless body. Unfortunately, as I had sus-pected, my father had passed away.

My mother had made it to the hospital and was with him when he took his last breath. Only the week before he had submitted his retirement documents to his job and was just sixty years old on the day of his death. The hospital cleared the room of other patients and allowed my family to say our last goodbyes. Though I suspect this was because they felt somewhat guilty for not doing enough to save him. The official cause of his death was a blood clot in his lungs. I had fought through a lot of tough days recently, but the grief I felt that day when I had to say goodbye to my father was the most emotionally draining. Mustering up the strength to explain to Cam that he would not see his "Crappa" again also took an emotional toll on me.

My father's funeral services were held at my parents' home. At his funeral I spoke with my relatives about memories of my time with him and all that he had taught me. I shared a story about the time I talked him into getting back on a motorcycle. While living in Oregon he had lost a friend who passed away in a motorcycle accident. Because of this he swore never to ride again. I had a Harley Davidson motorcycle, that I purchased with my overtime money, which I earned while working in custody facilities. I was no longer able to ride it due to my hand injury, and I routinely tried to talk him into taking it out, but he adamantly refused.

One day he had called to tell me he was coming to my home to see me. So, I quickly cleaned up the bike, rolled it out of the garage and into the driveway. When he arrived, I walked to the driveway to greet him. During our conversation I interrupted his speech and stated that I would be right back and began to walk toward the house. As I made my way to the front door I turned and said, "The key is in the bike if you want to check it out. I haven't been able to run it lately, and it's been sitting too long."

From inside the house, I heard the bike's motor start. I was ecstatic to hear this, in hopes that he would ride it. After making my way to the front yard, a mile-long smile spread across my face. I could see that both the bike and my father were absent from the driveway. A moment later I heard the noise of the bike's big v-twin motor as it was coming down the street. Wearing the biggest grin I have ever seen; he rode right past the house on the bike. Thanks to the courage he showed that afternoon, for the rest of my days, that is exactly how I will remember him.

With the funeral behind her, my mother was left living in the house alone. The memories of my father were too much for her to bear, so she made the decision to sell the family home. The task of cleaning out the house and getting it ready for sale was left to my brothers and me. We moved my mother's belongings and finished cleaning up the house. The house sold and she used the proceeds from the sale to purchase a small condominium. Preparing my mother's home to sell made me realize that because of my divorce, I would soon be forced to do the same. I didn't want to sell Cam's childhood home, but I knew I would have no choice.

Just as my mother settled into her new place, I put my own home on the market. I told my soon-to-be ex-wife that she could have all the equity in our home, if she would agree to equal custody of Cam. She agreed, and to me it was more than worth the money not to risk custody of my son. I knew that if I wanted, I could bring up her past and fight for full custody. But I felt a battle was not fare to everyone involved, especially Cam.

It was difficult to let the house go, but I was thankful for the five years we were able to occupy the home. The house was small, about the same size as the one my mother had just sold. But it had a pool which formed some of Cam's best childhood memories.

Swimming with his friends on a hot summer day had always put a smile on his face, and I knew this would have made my grandmother proud. This place had provided stability for Cam, and I was grateful that we were able to give this to him. I could not afford to buy another home on just my sheriff pension, so my quest was now to find a new career.

CHAPTER SIX

Ages 30 to 40

The injury that caused the premature ending to my deputy career, occurred while I was on duty. Because of this the department was now responsible for providing me with training toward a replacement career. Knowing this the department offered to pay a small amount toward my education in a field of my choice. I chose to attend a school for residential property inspections. My plan was to obtain an inspector's certificate so that I could seek out another government position as a building inspector.

Upon the completion of my training, I began a search for job openings with local government agencies. I found an opening in my old hometown city in the high desert of Southern California, where my parents had lived. Returning to work in the area wasn't the ideal situation; I hadn't cared for it since the day my parents originally moved there from Oregon, and I wasn't looking forward to moving back. However, the new position paid well and would allow me to purchase a home for Cam and me to start over. My duties would include the enforcement of property municipal codes. Not my dream occupation, of course, but again one that offered financial stability and the benefits I needed.

My initial interview for the position was with the department director named Pamela. Included in the panel were the human resources manager, and a third-party developer not employed by the city. It felt like more of an interrogation than an evaluation. Although grueling, over all it went well, that is apart from one odd question. The question was posed to me by Pamela. Toward the end of the interview she asked, "If you were an animal, what kind of animal would you like to be?" I stopped for a moment to ponder her question and then responded, "An animal that is free to roam the earth as he pleases, unrestrained by walls and borders."

Hearing my answer, she took the opportunity to belittle me by stating, "You mean like a rodent." I wanted to say, "No, not like you with your long gray-haired ponytail, resembling the tail of a squirrel." Fortunately, I was able to suppress the derogatory remark I wanted to make and instead replied with, "No, more like an eagle." I could tell she was mystified by my response, so I continued. "When I was younger my father took me to the Redwood Forest. There I learned that in rough weather, eagles are lifted above the storm where they can rest their wings. I like the idea of being able to see my way through trouble and find the peace above."

The next thing that should have come out of my mouth was, "Eagles soar over hardships and attack from above while rodents only steal and hide," though once again thankfully, I was able to restrain myself. It must have worked because I ended up with the job. The day I left the city's employment, my mother presented me with one of her homemade framed picture puzzles as a gift. The picture in the puzzle is of an eagle soaring through the sky, and seeing it I thought,

Wow, how fitting. It wasn't long before I started to see that accepting the position may not have been in my best interest.

Short in stature with a slim build, Pamela was always professionally dressed. Her daily uniform consisted of a business suit, with her hair pulled back in a ponytail, like that of a gymnast, which she always wanted to be. She was around the same age as my older brother at the time I met her. She had an elegant way of displaying her very disgruntled demeanor; She possessed all the virtues I disliked and none of the vices I admired. Her vices included vanity and an insatiable pride in her own achievements. Her motivations appeared to develop through greed; she had no time for others unless they had something to offer her. With an often-stated unapologetic dislike for animals and children, she reminded me of the character Cruella de Vil from the movie *One Hundred and One Dalmatians*.

Having no interest in impressing others, I somehow surprisingly earned a promotion from Pamela, which I later discovered was due to ulterior motives. I had been performing code inspections for a year, when I received the promotion to a supervisory position. My new role in the department would encompass the management of city-owned property. I was at first excited about my new duties, though it turned out working for Pamela as a supervisor was much more stressful.

Along with the new position, I became the honorary recipient of her empathy-resistant approach to management. She held the expectation that her supervisors were to possess a mentality of servility. Her employees were often subjected to tantrums of yelling and swearing when she couldn't get her way. She became well known for her use of profanity. In fact, many of her employees would joke that if we put out a cuss jar for her, we would probably be able to run a laundry mat from the proceeds.

My training in situational de-escalation as a deputy, provided me with some advantages, when dealing with Pamela and her hostile behavior. Though this was not the case with many of her other employees, who lacked resilience. Pamela's constant staff pressure resulted in department employee turnover. Her drive went far beyond passion to the point that it almost personified evil, and yet she seemed to relish it. She had very little compassion for others, and the working environment in the city provided plenty of fuel for that fire.

After being employed with the city for over a year, I was witness to the modus operandi she was subjected to. This aspect helped me gain some perspective on how her overly authoritative demeanor developed. I saw that this city appeared to be very bold and aggressive when it came to bending the rules. To keep the council happy, city management discovered creative ways to develop programs that provided incentives to local bureaucrats. This would often place stress on employees in their attempts to make these pet projects appear legitimate.

City employees were expected to be subservient; they were constantly forced to appease the unethical funding requests of their bosses. It was as though the city was just their personal piggy bank, with access to a constant supply of local public tax revenue to do with as they pleased. Special-project funding requests were not uncommon and often took precedence. After observing this, Pamela's job-related belligerent personality issues started to make more sense to me. Although Pamela was not the only one affected by this, a subject of which details I will expand upon.

This city had a high crime rate and rampant use of drugs, causing citizens reduced civic interest, which provided an easy target for dishonest officials. The city had become so saturated with crime and political corruption that it couldn't be wrung out with any level of corroborated investigation. Crime was so frequent here that only a few of the elected officials and top administration dared to even reside in the city limits. City officials, including the city manager, directors, and the mayor, could all afford to live in more affluent surrounding areas. It astonished me how outright hypocritical these exurbanite city leaders were. Preaching to buy locally, while utilizing the support from a public-supplied income, to provide themselves with better lives elsewhere.

RIDING

My own commute to my new job combined with my elevated duties made life difficult for Cam and me. I was renting a place near my old home and wanted to move closer to my job. After my divorce I lacked the financial means to live outside the city. Because of this I chose the best area within the city limits that I could afford, where Cam could hopefully spend his teenage years. It was the year 2008, and the housing market was crashing, which made it easier for me to purchase a home.

The market allowed me to find a large new house that fit within my budget. The house was on the west side of the city away from the criminal element. Upon showing our new home to Cam, he thoroughly explored every room and gave his exuberant approval. He was eleven at the time, and I felt that after all he had been through with me and his mom, he deserved a nice place to live. I had borrowed the five percent down payment from my mother to purchase the property.

Cam enjoyed our new home, but like me when my parents moved from Oregon, he had difficulties adjusting to being displaced from his childhood friends. I enrolled Cam into a new school and attempted to get him involved in some local after-school activities. Although keeping him busy became a worrisome task. He had developed a medical issue with his legs, which prevented him from participating in many sports. A lack of proper circulation to his lower extremities, was causing him pain, and making it burdensome for him to walk. I was desperate to find him something he could do to keep his mind occupied and would be therapeutic for his legs.

The answer to this came in the form of my old hobby, bicycle racing. Racing helped give my childhood purpose, and I hoped it would do the same for him. With the goal of securing his interest in bikes, I purchased the nicest one I could find. His favorite color was green, and I was able to find a bright green bicycle made by the company Redline. On the drive home from picking up the bike, I was anxious to see his reaction, hoping it would inspire him. Unable to hold the surprise, I presented the bike to Cam as soon as I arrived. To my relief, upon seeing the bike he exclaimed, "This is the best gift ever!" My plan had worked. Just like when I saw my first bike, the attraction for him was instant.

With luck on our side, we found a bicycle racetrack located within two miles of our new home. The dirt track was newly developed and available to the public. It was open daily and offered different experience levels to compete in. The racetrack was well designed and maintained, which attracted the attention of riders from around the nation. It had everything a racer needed, from a repair shop to a snack bar and even a grandstand area for an audience.

Cam was excited to ride with the other kids and wanted to go every chance possible. The more he practiced, the better at riding he became, starting at a novice level and quickly advancing to an expert. Riding helped his legs grow stronger, and the races he won helped to develop his confidence. His enthusiasm made me want to support him any way I could. A year into the hobby, I had already bought Cam three different race bikes. The last one was a very special bike I bought just for the annual state championships.

Because of the location of the track, the racing commission decided the championships were to be held in our hometown. The track was prepared, and a new state-of-the-art start gate was installed, for the annual national championship races. Cam would now be able to compete, in the nationals, on the same track he practiced on every day. I knew there would be a lot of quality racers in attendance for this race. This made me concerned that Cam may not perform well against the more experienced racers. I feared he may become disappointed if defeated, I hoped the new bike and the home track advantage would help.

CHAMPION

After bringing his new race bike onto the track for him to practice, I could see he was battling to control it. It was obviously too big for him; I had been a little overzealous in its purchase. Seeing this, I decided to take after my father, and set out to build him one. Utilizing the best parts I could find, I assembled the lightest, fastest bike possible. I gave the bike to Cam and told him, "This is the best I can do, bud. The rest will be up to you." He took the bike for a test run, and returned with a smile and said, "I can do this dad."

The bike had restored his confidence, and his words made me recall how I felt when my father first handed me the Green Machine. I knew moments like this that evoked pleasant memories of past experiences were to be cherished. These moments don't come often enough; in life, it seems our troubled times are more easily recalled. The feeling of pride I gained through the confidence I heard in Cam's voice, I owed to lessons from my father. His actions always demonstrated how these precious fleeting moments are earned through supporting others.

The national championship races were held on a hot California summer day. Upon our arrival at the event, I could see that Cam was nervous but excited. Hundreds of riders and spectators were in attendance, along with dozens of vendors from all over the state. Cam was anxious and could hardly wait to get on to the track. As soon as I parked, he ran to the back of my truck to retrieve his race bike. He had already donned his helmet and racing gear before I could even complete the registration process.

The prerequisite to race in the finals was to win a qualifying race. Though considering what he had to overcome with his legs, just completing a race would be an accomplishment for him. With a little struggle, to my astonishment, he made it into the finals. The final riders' names were placed in a drawing for lane choice; most riders wanted the middle lane. There was a total of ten riders with him in the race, and Cam didn't fare that well with the drawing as he drew the inside lane. In my attempt to dismiss his concern and instead induce encouragement, I issued a small white lie to him; saying, "Don't worry about the lane bud, it's the best one, where all the winners came from."

Cam appeared uneasy as he lined up at the gate next to the current national champion rider. Like my father did to me, I told him to lean forward because the front end of the bike may come up when the gate drops. Hearing my voice, he leaned on the handlebars, pushing the front wheel of the bike into the gate. The starting buzzer began its countdown and the expression on Cam's face changed from frightened to intense.

The buzzer sounded, the gate dropped, and to my complete disbelief, he got out first. I thought, *well, that's good, now at least he has a chance to be on the podium.* Evidently, the current champion rider saw the same thing and turned his bike straight toward Cam, trying to cut him off. Just before the two bikes collided, Cam glanced over and saw the other rider. Seeing that the other rider was coming his way, he instinctively leaned his bike in the direction of the champion. The two bikes slammed into each other and Cam was able to absorb the hit.

Cams anticipation of the impending impact allowed him to maintain control of his bike. Though the same was not true of the champion. The collision sent him and his bike over the track's embankment. In the process of proceeding off the track, he cut off several other riders. This helped to eliminate some of Cam's other competitors and enabled him to retain his lead.

Appreciating the gravity of the moment was not easy for me as I was still trying to digest what I had just witnessed. Not wanting to miss him at the end, I leaped from my seat and off the bleachers, running toward the finish line. Unfortunately, in the process I had to jump over a few other spectators causing me to spill my soda on them. I didn't have time to stop and apologize, so I could only hope they would forgive me, and understand the reason for my excitement. When I got to the end of the racetrack, I could see that he was still out in front and pedaling as fast as his legs could go. The look on his face showed that he was as shocked to be out in front as I was to see him there. His intensity was now replaced with a mouth-wide-open look of amazement.

Cam flew across the finish line first, just ahead of the next two riders. Crossing the finish line, he was traveling so fast I had to yell out to him "hit the brakes!", just so he wouldn't run into the concession stand. I don't believe he wanted to stop pedaling. He jumped off his bike, ran up to me and asked, "Did I win?" to which I replied, "Yes son, of course you did." With our heads held high, Cam and I proudly made our way to the trophy stand to retrieve his well-deserved first-place trophy.

On our way to the stand, we walked by the rider that hit him. The rider was covered in dirt; while pushing his bike he scowled at Cam as we passed. I told Cam, "Don't worry, he is upset at losing, not at you." The first-place trophy stood just as tall as he did, but he wouldn't allow me to help him carry it. He couldn't be prouder of it and would rather let the base of it drag on the ground in the dirt than let someone else carry it for him.

Being there to witness the smile on his face, while he dragged his trophy around, made every difficult moment to that point of my life worth it. I was always afraid that he could cause more damage to his injured legs while riding. But entering him into that national race turned out to be one of the best decisions I had ever made. I guess we will never realize the gifts that await us if we allow fear to influence our decisions.

OFFICIALS

The time I spent with my son at the racetrack gave me the mental break I desperately needed. Without this, my daily routine of tolerating the mundane world of government employment would not have been possible. The monotony was routinely interrupted by the unpleasant constant verbal attacks courtesy of my boss, Pamela. It was now clear her anger had evolved from the unethical funding requests of officials. Purging herself she would distribute her hostility onto her employees, infecting the work environment with her anger and mutating others into additional victims.

Personnel, such as Pamela, quickly discovered that executive staff and elected officials had the expectation of being praised and treated as royalty. Going along with their wishes was necessary for employment regardless of any possible legal repercussions. Though compliance could also lead to potential personal benefits for the employee. For these employees the line between right and wrong seemed to quickly fade when it came to appeasing these officials. Requests would involve the hiring of specific people for a certain job or approving a consultant contract that would benefit them.

Officials in the city also had a special talent for making their projects appear to benefit the citizens. They often had their own selfish agenda when taking office; campaign promises seldom seemed to be a priority. Sadly, many who accepted these elected roles came from religious entities or were prominent business owners. They used their public image to gain access to the voters when marketing themselves for an elected position. After their election, they would then use their authority to complete their personal project goals.

Coming from a Christian household, I found the use of religion by executives to gain power the most disturbing. When I discussed this with my mom, she told me that religion was man-made. She stated that it had lost its meaning; it was used these days mostly by the corrupt to gain wealth and power and avoid taxes. This idea that someone could exploit a religious belief for personal gain was hard for me to accept. It seems to me this would be the true description of using God's name in vain. If my mom is right and heaven and hell do exist, I surely wouldn't want to be one of those preachers trying to explain their actions. Using divine motivation for self-serving behavior might be a tough one to talk your way out of.

Here the line between church and state was beyond blurred and these religious figures didn't mind being bowed to as a government official. Employees bowing to their needs and praising their efforts caused officials and executives' egos to grow. Operating unchecked, their egos continued to advance, to the point they felt invincible. Feeling empowered, they didn't act concerned about any repercussions from their unethical actions. It appeared as if they didn't even comprehend the existence of law, or possibly they felt they were above it. This made me wonder just how many other cities were allowed to operate in this way. After years of feeling the effects of their actions, I believe all elected officials should undergo extensive ethics training.

SPECIAL

As I previously mentioned, enacting the request from city officials came with a lot of benefits for personnel. Upon retirement, elected officials would provide compliant executive personnel with large gifts. These gifts came in the form of lucrative consultant contracts and increased salaries to bolster their public pensions. In expectation of this, executive employees would use creative methods to fund large parties for city officials and campaign donors.

The parties were instituted under the disguise of public events for the benefit of local citizens. This allowed them to use public funds and public property for such gatherings. These events would involve lots of free alcohol and activities like go-kart rides for officials, courtesy of the taxpayers. Consultants receiving large contracts from city officials would also provide paybacks. These amounted to providing free locations for City Christmas parties and other gatherings.

Although unequally, non-executive city employees were also rewarded for their compliance. These benefits came in the form of pay raises, administrative time off, and unearned supervisory titles. This process caused underqualified personnel to be placed into management positions. Some compliant employees were even allowed

109

to accompany elected officials on trips abroad. Trips like this were taken on the guise of creating city agreements and were of course also funded by public tax dollars.

Many employees hired into full-time, full-benefit jobs were done so out of authoritative influence. When the need arose, a position that did not exist would be invented and developed with specific employees in mind. The toleration of this process led to the presence of overpaid and unreliable government workers throughout the city. As a result, more qualified but overlooked applicants would quit, leading to higher attrition rates. This would cause the citizens to unknowingly suffer by not receiving proper services they paid for through their taxes. A nonproductive environment developed, protected by people concerned for their own futures and interests.

Due to this process overlooked personnel would sometimes use the knowledge of executives' misdeeds as leverage to gain positions for themselves. Influence used against officials might have consisted of evidence of wrong behavior, a payback favor, or possibly knowledge of sexual misconduct. In one such incident, a retired county worker was hired by the city for a newly created position. His name was Joe, and he happened to be an old friend of the city manager. Because of his connections, Joe was provided with an excessive salary for his qualifications and placed in charge of a department overseeing several employees.

Joe was a large man with the persona of a bully. Upon meeting him I felt insulted by his presence and found myself questioning the need for his existence. I felt only disdain for his offensive nature, he didn't appear to possess enough ethics to properly cross a street. When he spoke, his level of intellect sounded like he had never utilized his head for anything other than a hat rack. To me he was the type of person whose funeral I would not attend, although I would send a letter of approval.

The city manager, who gained his own position through nepotism, hired Joe as a supervisor, and then quickly created and promoted him to a new director's position. The new position was invented for him, and he was not required to apply or qualify for it. As with other positions, more qualified applicants were over-looked and not allowed to submit applications. After being placed in charge of his new department, Joe quickly became the defendant in three separate sexual harassment complaints and lawsuits from his employees.

At the time, I didn't know who it was more difficult to work with, Joe, Pamela or another employee from the city public works department. This other employee was a self-proclaimed abuser, as he admitted in a council meeting. In an awkward attempt at receiving their forgiveness, he stood before the council and professed to the abuse of his children. The council gladly obliged him with their acceptance of his apology. I shouldn't have been surprised at the city's acceptance of abusive employees, as there was a large popu-lation of registered sex offenders living here. Although Joe was too self-centered and arrogant to pull off this type of charade. He would never publicly admit to his misbehavior.

Working with Joe and observing his overtly obscene interac-tions with female employees, made me want to leave city employ-ment. I could only describe his actions as those of a womanizing narcissist. The lawsuits taken against the city from his harassment of his female staff, became common knowledge among other employ-ees through gossip. It was circulated that the city covered up the lawsuits by paying off the victims with public money and provid-ing them with promotions. The city moved the female employees to other departments and allowed Joe to keep his position. Even knowing how the city operated I still somewhat disbelieved the pure audacity displayed in achieving this outcome.

The truth of why Joe retained his job was revealed to me by Pamela. She informed me that Joe and the mayor had become friends when Joe worked for the county, and according to her, Joe had performed a favor for the mayor. From what I understood this favor involved the mayors wish to reduce the city's low-income residents. Since this is related to another city incident, I will continue discussing this in a subsequent chapter.

Pamela often spoke to me about the actions of executives and councilmen. She told me of back-door property deals and that it was common for executives to have affairs with their secretaries. It didn't take me long to figure out why she routinely divulged this type of information to me. My own ignorance was at fault for not seeing that she had an attraction to me, although the feeling was not mutual. She probably liked me because I was the only one who could deal with her violent outburst, but now I was aware of the possible reason behind my promotion.

PRESSURE

Learning of the lawsuits Joe had generated, the mayor was not concerned. After all, it was not his money and not the first time they were sued. In a statement, he once professed that as far as he was concerned, it was his city, and everyone worked for him. He was the lead gray squirrel in charge. In my view, the greediest oldest and grayest of them all, whose arrogance was only outweighed by his ignorance. He had made a fortune in the pockets of others, which required him to employ a personal bodyguard. He liked to show off his wealth and owned more cars than he could drive, most costing as much as many people's houses. At the least his level of gluttony was inferior to none I had seen before. His pride made him very unapproachable, therefore I had never personally met him, although I didn't regret not shaking his hand. I recall, during one of Pamela's tirades, she exclaimed that the mayor was a publicly self-admitted cocaine user and had at one time dealt cocaine from a bar he had owned.

The added cost of attorneys, exorbitant directors' salaries, and raiding of the city budget for pet programs, caused reductions to be made to non-executive employee salaries and benefits. Announcements delivered to employees, regarding the city's inability to afford raises, included the excuse of reduced tax increment income. But the personnel facing cutbacks were aware of the real reasons. Executives would boldly make these cuts while directing their staff to give out million-dollar contracts to friends and relatives of officials. One such contract was for a small plane to fly over the city and look for criminals. The plane chosen was said to be operated by one of the official's relatives. These officials portrayed themselves as heroes to the public for signing such contracts. Though the real heroes were the personnel who had to tolerate the consequences of their brash, corrupt actions.

Like many employees, the executives' prejudiced actions had a direct impact on my own career. I was also passed over on several positions that went to less qualified employees and suffered from a change in my benefits. By complaining I would take the chance of being fired. The other option was to walk away from the pressure of this career. Though this would mean leaving an irreplaceable pension and entering an uncertain future. Becoming reliant on the government financially to access life sustaining necessities was the trap set by the squirrels. As with many welfare recipients, most public employees were not willing to jeopardize their income and therefore remained trapped in this system.

These were not the only reasons provided to me for seeking new employment, but finding a replacement career would prove not possible. I believe Pamela may have faced a similar dilemma as it was now clear that the constant job pressure did get to her. I'm not saying this was the only cause of her demeanor, but when combined with her sexual frustration, a whirlwind of tantrums was created. Most of which was unfortunately directed toward me, due to my fending off her many advances. This also developed into her jealousy of me working with other female employees.

Her behavior eventually left me with no choice but to make a complaint and hire an attorney. The complaint was dismissed by the human resources director, who then threatened to have me fired if I did not drop my lawsuit. My lawyer advised me that, although it had been approved by the state, the lawsuit offered me no protection from being fired. I was forced to pay my attorney fees and dismiss it.

Another supervisor had witnessed the harassment I endured, although she had her own reasons for not saying anything. She had been involved romantically with one of her subordinates and knew that the city would use that against her if she voiced her opinion over Pamela's treatment of me. Though my complaint was not taken seriously, it did at least halt Pamela's inappropriate behavior toward me. I no longer had to listen to her stories about her husband's impotence or be told by her which female employees I was allowed to work with. I was thankful for this as it made my job more tolerable for the time being.

The harassment complaint I submitted against Pamela was not her first, nor would it be the last. Soon after my complaint, another similar one was made against her. This complaint came from a supervisor named Kevin, who would eventually become my new boss. Kevin had more influence on the executive staff than I did, so his complaint was investigated and verified. This new complaint caused the city to force her to accept a mandated retirement—with full benefits, of course. They couldn't just fire her as she still knew where all the officials' skeletons were buried, and they couldn't afford to burn a bridge with her. Besides, they knew that by allowing her previous actions, they had already set a standard of acceptance. One thing was certain: from the time I met her till the time she left, the wrinkles between her eyebrows had significantly increased.

CHAPTER SEVEN

Ages 40 to 50

Due to her departure, significant adjustments were forced upon Pamela's old department, which I was a part of. The city had begun to evolve, though not for the better. Peter was the new city manager, and he decided to reorganize employee positions. Peter was a large man in his mid-forties. He was reportedly hired for one reason: he was willing to do whatever the mayor and council wanted. He had a jovial but vindictive personality. In listening to him communicate, I noticed that he strayed from the use of words that others might need to look up in a dictionary. It seemed he attempted to make up for his lack of command over the English language, by implementing a passive-aggressive type of humor into his conversations.

With Peter now in charge, hand-picked employees were again beginning to be moved to newly created positions. As with Joe's promotion, these supervisor spots were never offered to the public or to other employees. The personnel posted to these promotional assignments were being done so as favors. Unfortunately, as before, many of the employees who benefited from these jobs lacked the knowledge required to fulfill their duties.

Part of Peter's restructuring involved the breaking up of Pamela's old department. Half of her employees were placed under Barbara, a newly hired director and friend to a councilman who was also a local preacher. The other half were placed under Daniel, a recently promoted manager. Before being appointed to his position, Daniel was employed by the city at the same supervisory level that I was. Daniel was also very close friends with the previous city manager. This connection made it easy for the previous manager to ask Peter to supply Daniel with the new position.

At the time of his promotion there were other employees, more qualified for the position than he was, including myself. Several of the neglected employees were upset at not being offered a chance to apply for the new positions being handed out. When they made complaints, the employees were told by Peter, "You are lucky to have a seat." This was common; he would often tell employees that if they did not like something, they could leave.

The position given to Daniel was not a new one as many others were. It had been advertised before; at which time I had applied. Though it was retracted and placed on hold to make room for the hiring of Joe. In response to my application, the human resources department supplied me with an acceptance letter, which I was still in possession of. The letter promised me a chance at the job upon its reinstatement. Since I had this evidence and was already on their bad side due to my complaint against Pamela. I decided to share the letter with the city and inquire about an interview. Upon seeing the letter, the new human resources manager denied my request and stated that she would simply change the title of the position. Underhanded, yes, but it was quick thinking on her part, although she never did change the title.

Because of my complaint about Daniels promotion, being deposited under the supervision of Barbara was now their only option for me. There were twelve personnel placed under Barbara, of which I was the only male. It didn't take long for me to learn that I was not in a favorable position, Barbara was partial the female employees. A female herself and now in her mid-thirties, she had a very headstrong, competitive personality. Handpicked for her position her sights were set on being the next city manager. Like in my scenario, I knew of another employee that was in line for her director's spot. He had also submitted a complaint about Barbara's promotion, but like Pamela, was forced from city employment. This should have acted as my warning not to complain about the position given to Daniel, that I was overlooked for.

SURGERY

While dealing with the man-made chaos of city work, I was also trying to help Cam safely navigate his high school years. There is no beauty in man-made chaos, but there is in the chaos of parenting a child. I did my best to stay close to Cam, hoping to be there when he needed me. In doing so, I could see that some of the peer pressure from unscrupulous students was influencing his decisions. Thinking back on the wrestler who was injured in my high school parking lot, I knew I had to step in. After deliberating on how to assist him with his new dilemma. I settled on the idea of interjecting by utilizing my father's parenting trick of distraction through nature.

With all the strain from my work and this pressure on Cam from his new school, we both desperately needed to get away. I decided to plan a vacation, and knew there was no better way to help my son than to spend time sharing with him the wonders of nature. Since I hadn't been able to take much time off while working under the thumb of my old boss, Pamela, I had plenty of vacation time. I informed my new boss, Barbara, that I would be taking a two-week vacation with my son. It was summer and Cam was on break from school, and he loved the water, so I booked us a white-water rafting trip on the American River. Cam was at first very resistant to the idea of the trip. But with a little convincing—and by that, I mean bribery, I was able to get him to go.

It was a long drive from our house to the river, and staying in a tent on the riverbank was not that comfortable. Because of this Cam complained the whole time until we were on the water. I knew once we were in the boats everything would change for him. Like going on your first roller-coaster or for a ride on a Jet Ski, it's extremely difficult to complain when your sense of survival is overwhelmed. As I suspected, my father's method worked perfectly, and after the first day on the river Cam could not stop talking about the rapids. The excitement he expressed while describing the exhilaration he felt revealed that his high school worries were now gone. My mental picture of him on the inflatable boat, smiling and holding his paddle over his head while triumphantly yelling "yes," will be lodged in my mind forever.

Cam's youthful joy allowed me to unlock my mind from the influence of the daily disparity my work provided to me. This freed me from my own discouraging thoughts long enough to concentrate on something much more important, his development. I was able to teach him many things he would not learn in school. Such as how new experiences could help him grow and provide him with mental survival skills. Though it was his own tenacity that saw him through to his high school graduation.

Setting aside a little extra from each paycheck, I saved for his higher education. Upon his graduation, I gave him the option of college or a job. He smartly chose college, and we ended up settling for one he found out of state. The choice of where to go to school came down to the cost. The school he chose to attend happened to be in the state of Texas, where his mom now lived. Although I was against him being around her influence, it made economic sense for him to live with her while attending school. Sending my son off to live in another state was difficult, but I knew it was necessary.

Another necessity entered my life just after my son's departure. While on our rafting trip, I noticed my reoccurring lower back pain had worsened. I had unfortunately suffered from lower back pain for some time and was told by a doctor that it required surgery. My doctor advised me that a disk in my lower back had disintegrated and needed to be fused. I believe that the damage to my back occurred during the fight with the suspect in the incident that caused my hand injury. Although the damage may have occurred years earlier, I was now stuck requesting that the operation be covered under my current health insurance.

Once I found a surgeon capable of performing the operation, I submitted a coverage authorization request to my insurance. Only days after I received approval, I was notified by the city that it would be changing carriers due to cost. In checking with the new insurance company, I found that they would not cover this type of surgery. If I was to have my back fixed, I would need to have the procedure before my work changed policy carriers. This meant that for it to be covered it would have to be completed before the end of the year, which was now less than a month away.

The surgeon's last available date for a procedure was December 23rd of 2019, which I quickly secured. I had the operation done in a hospital three hours from my home and spent Christmas Day that year in a recovery room. Thoughtfully, my mom had flown in and came to visit me the day after the surgery, on Christmas Eve. Although unfortunately, she was forced to leave early as a bad storm was entering the city that night. Because of this, I spent the next day alone in a hospital bed, which turned out to be the loneliest day of my life.

Christmas time for me growing up was filled with lots of gifts and spent in the company of my family. This one I would have to spend without them, a situation only compounded by being in pain and surrounded by strangers. The dark cloud that had settled upon me was lifted by a very polite young nurse, who assisted me with using the phone so I could talk to my son. When you are feeling at your worst, it is sometimes the simplest gesture from a kind stranger that can keep your spirits alive. My recovery was long and difficult and most of the time, I was in extreme pain. There is nothing like a life-altering physical ailment to help you appreciate your health and develop empathy for the plight of others with similar issues.

Since Cam was now in school and was not able to fly back to assist with my recovery, my mother had decided to fly out to be with me. She had moved to Louisiana years before to be closer to her sister, and said she needed a little vacation time. I am sure she used the vacation statement as an excuse, but I was relieved to know she would be coming. Regardless of her reason, having my mom around was comforting. I was against taking medication, and our talks kept me from thinking about the pain. She didn't stay long, only a couple of weeks, but her company was helpful.

During my mother's stay, we reminisced over events of my childhood and shared stories of my father. She commented on how much Cam resembled him and how my father loved to drive the car he and I built together. As a teenager, my father owned a 1965 Pontiac

GTO, which he constantly bragged about. He lost the car in an accident and often spoke of replacing it. I was able to find one that needed restoration, which I purchased as a gift for his fiftieth birthday. We spent the next ten years restoring the car together. The restoration was completed just a year before he passed away at the age of sixty. Tears ran down my mother's face as she described the pride, he took in driving the car.

It was obviously difficult for her to see her son in pain, though I am sure our conversations were as much a distraction for her as they were for me. My mother was with me during all the hard times in my life. She was there for me while I was in the Army, when I was shot, and when I was getting a divorce. She always made me a priority, and I was very thankful for her. Although like with many parents and children, my mother and I did not always get along. She grew up in a generation where smoking and drinking were commonplace. Following the precedents set by her parents, she had often turned to consuming alcohol as a coping mechanism, which made her irritable. I have no idea how difficult it was raising three boys with little money, so I had long since forgiven her for the methods she used to deal with her issues when I was a child.

Upon my mother's departure and without Cam, I relied mainly upon the help from my new girlfriend, Diane. Diane was also previously married but had no children of her own. We met the year before at a concert and are complete opposites, but our personalities seem to complement each other. Even though she is more of an extrovert, and I am more of an introvert, we still share many similar interests, such as rock music. Diane's companionship was pleasant, and I appreciated having her there to help me. However, Due to her own work schedule, she was not able to stay with me full time during my healing process.

To occupy my mind, I kept in touch with several coworkers. In one of the conversations, a fellow employee told me about his theory on the city changing insurance carriers. He thought their reason was not due to the expense, as they claimed, but was because of the insurance broker. He explained that from his understanding, the broker's profit was higher with the new insurance company. Apparently, the broker had ties with some of the council members and the city changed insurance carriers due to influence. Hearing this, I was glad I was able to have the operation completed and behind me.

BOSS

Over a month had passed since my mother's departure before I could drive my car again and return to work. My new boss, Barbara, was not the least bit concerned about my recovery. I would often overhear her asking her female employees how they were feeling, but upon my return, she said nothing to me. Her only concern was what my job duties were and how I could help her. Barbara was new to working with government programs and was mainly interested in knowing about my projects. As she had requested, I went about documenting my job duties and current projects for her.

After reviewing my submission, Barbara had a lot of questions for me. Answering her questions and explaining the city programs to her, turned out to be an exhausting process. In her attempts to appear knowledgeable, she gave very little feedback. Her lack of response showed that this was the first time she had heard the information I was providing. This also made it difficult to tell if she was grasping the basics of the programs. While I was speaking to her, she would become overwhelmed, often cutting me off to end the conversation. Barbara's style of management was somewhat familiar to me.

Most managers I met with council connections had the tendency to display an entitled behavior.

Barbara devoted most of her time and attention to her female employees—that is, until she needed something from me. Her actions toward me were those of complete disrespect; they bordered on being rude and reminded me of a spoiled child. My request for information regarding the financing of programs would go unanswered, and I was often left out of department meetings. It was almost as if she was purposely trying to make me uncomfortable. She would even ignore my presence while walking by me in a hallway.

Several times I caught myself trying to figure out if I had possibly done something wrong, but I knew that wasn't the case, as I was always polite to her. The only thing I could come up with was either she didn't like males, she didn't like ex-cops, or she was told to get rid of me. I believed it was the latter, and maybe it was easier for her to not think of me as human if she knew I was to be laid off. I guess after she finished squeezing me for program information, I was to be her sacrificial lamb, her method of earning her new position. Barbara's poor treatment of me escalated systematically, as if it was a planned attempt to strip me of my integrity.

At one point she moved me from a large, spacious office to an area that had been previously used as a closet. I felt like I had become the character from the movie *Office Space*, who was moved to the basement with his red stapler. Originally designed for storage, my new office had an emergency light that constantly emitted an intense buzzing noise. I asked if the light could be fixed, but my request was made in vain. In my attempts to avoid the noise of my office light, I began to do more field work, conducting inspections of my city projects. When she discovered this, Barbara abruptly ended my field trips, confiscating my city vehicle with no explanation.

Months after occupying my new closet/office, I noticed the buzzing sound did not go away after I left work. The noise had lingering power; I had left the office, but the noise did not leave me. A constant annoying buzzing in my ears had now developed. I again attempted to contact Barbara about fixing the light; though her secretary advised me that she was now working from home. I knew that I had to do something about the persistent issue that had now developed in my ears. I decided it was time to call the city human resources department and make an official complaint. I advised the human resources manager of how I was being treated, and of the constant buzzing in my ears from the broken office light. I didn't expect much to come of my complaint, but to my surprise she decided to investigate.

The manager conducted a month-long investigation and determined that Barbara had indeed treated me unfairly. I was moved back to my original office and provided medical assistance for the issue with my ears. Barbara was advised of the findings and decided to leave city employment. Before leaving she came to my office, looked me straight in the eye, and said, "I have decided to resign my position at the city due to your complaint." I was at first shocked at this turn of events; my previous experience with the city suggested they would just let her actions slide. I thought that maybe, just maybe, things were changing in the city.

CHANGE

It didn't take long for me to be proved wrong about the city changing for the better. Upon Barbara's exit, the department was once again broken up, and this time I was placed under Kevin. Kevin was the same guy who had made the harassment complaint causing Pamela's forced retirement. Unfortunately, he too had very little experience working with city programs and would require a lot of training on my part to bring him up to speed. He had an easygoing personality, he always listened, asked lots of questions, and wanted to learn. Though his laid-back, gullible style made him an easy target for more powerful city personnel to take advantage of. His main influence came from the city attorney.

Barbara had previously worked extensively with the attorney and befriended her, by providing her with many city-billable hours. Therefore, the attorney would not be thrilled about the news of Barbara's exit. My understanding was that the attorney and Barbara were still in communication. This meant that she was aware I was the reason for Barbara's departure, and due to me she would now need to find an alternative method of creating billable hours. Her opportunity to make up for the loss of Barbara came in the form of Kevin. Having the attorney in Kevin's ear would complicate my working relationship with him. Knowing I was the cause of Barbara's exit, she would most likely want to oppose my views vicariously through Kevin.

One afternoon while in Kevin's office, I overheard him talking on the phone with the city attorney. The subject of the conversation was a project that I oversaw. The project they were discussing operated under the city's redevelopment program. It was designed to redistribute city-owned and rehabilitated single-family residences. The purpose was to assist low-income individuals in the purchase of these now-occupiable properties. The acquisition and disposition of city-owned properties fell under my job duties, and this was therefore a project under my purview.

Sensing the frustration in Kevin's voice while discussing the project's details with the attorney, it was clear that he was having difficulty grasping its objective. I stayed and waited for his conversation to end so that I might help him on how best to handle the situation. Once he was off the phone, he turned and asked me to explain to him the project functions. I advised him that the city had obtained federal funds to purchase and rehabilitate several hundred dilapidated single-family homes in the city. I told him that the federal contract supplying the funds had stipulations on the methods of distribution. I further explained that the funds could only be used to purchase and rehabilitate specific identified properties and then to assist in reselling them to people of low income.

Continuing with our conversation, I informed him that under the program, each new buyer had to be approved to purchase a redistributed city home. To be approved through the program, the buyer was required to submit their income information to the city just as they would for a home loan. I would then compare the buyer's income to the low-income affordability worksheet provided in the funding contract. If the buyer's income level did not surpass the max income allowed by the worksheet, we would assist them in the purchase of a city owned program home.

Kevin asked me, "If the new owner resells the home, will it be required to remain a low-income occupied property—and if so, how do we confirm that?"

I replied, "Yes, upon each purchase, the buyers are required to sign a restriction document that is recorded on the property's title."

I then explained that when the property is resold, the title company will see the recorded restriction and contact us for instructions. After this we request to see the new buyer's income documents. If the new buyer qualifies, the restriction stays on the deed when it is transferred. Though if the new buyer does not qualify, the restriction will need to be removed. To be removed the recorded restriction requires the seller to pay a fee to the city for its removal from the deed. This fee would come in the form of a percentage of their equity in the property upon sale.

Kevin then asked, "If the new buyer does not qualify, what is the cost to the seller to remove the restriction from the deed?"

I replied, according to the contract, the cost the seller would be forced to pay to remove the restriction would run about forty five percent, of their equity in the property. The amount of equity to be paid to the city by the seller as stated in the restriction is based on the number of years of ownership.

Kevin seemed to grasp the concept of city property disposition much faster than Barbara had. I was also glad he did not inquire about the more complicated acquisition and rehabilitation process. I lacked the energy to properly explain the procedures required under the rehabilitation agreements, for collecting and reporting contractor payroll documents to confirm compliance with the prevailing wage determination. As it was, I already had to describe to him the difference between real and personal property.

Several days after our discussion, Kevin came to me and handed me a document from the city attorney's office. While handing me the document, he said, "When we are income-qualifying new program home buyers, per the city attorney, we are now required to use this affordability worksheet, developed by her office." Glancing at the new document, I noticed right away that the income amounts were lower than the original ones in the projects funding contract.

Using this new worksheet, a buyer would now need an even lower income to qualify for the program. Adversely, because of the increase in property values, the new low-income qualified buyer would not make enough to get a purchase loan. The seller would then be forced to sell to a non-program qualified buyer, whose income was high enough to get a loan. Selling to a non-qualified buyer would in turn cause the seller to pay the city for the restriction to be removed from their deed. Many sellers with program-restricted homes would now be paying up to forty five percent of their equity to the city upon resale. The payoffs to the city would be substantial, and the new incoming funds would no longer be covered by the agreement use requirement.

This was all a bit complicated, but to sum it up, the city would be taking money from citizens by changing the terms of their agreements, without proper authorization. Voicing my opinion, I told Kevin that this was not right, to which he replied, "Use the attorney's worksheet. It is less work for you and more money for the city." I advised him that the program agreement requires us to use the program worksheet, and that this is potentially stealing from the sellers. Kevin replied, "This is what the city attorney wants. She told the city manager it was a good way to bring in money and reduce employee time, and he agreed."

It was difficult to believe what I was hearing, and I don't think Kevin fully understood what he was saying, though I had no choice but to comply. I made several complaints to Kevin's supervisor and human resources that this new process was not right. My complaints this time, though, were ignored as the process had been mandated by the city attorney. Part of the new process was a requirement that she would have to review each transaction. Which was evident of her ulterior motives, because this of course created more billable hours for her. Kevin wasn't bothered by this, as he felt her cost was covered by the extra funds, received through her required changes to the project. Her taking over the program also removed one more of my job duties, which brought me back to the suspicion of her trying to eliminate my position.

After the project changes were implemented, more and more each day I saw attempts to outsource and streamline my workload. Every conversation Kevin had with the city attorney seemed to result in inquiries about my duties. His responses to my questions about this became abrupt and short. As her influence on him grew, I could almost see Kevin's appearance change. His eyes began to narrow and turn cold, and his movements quickened, not unlike those of the squirrels just outside my office window. The attorney had provided him with claws and a nut to use them on, which unfortunately happened to be me.

The housing market was on the rise, and property equities started to increase along with the sales of program houses. This caused the payments to the city, mandated by the attorney, to become more significant. Once she saw that the implementation of her new plan was well received and prosperous, she set her sights on other city projects. Slowly, I witnessed programs transformed, and not to the benefit of the public. Changes made to carefully developed programs, out of bureaucratic interference, often leads to harmful outcomes. A case in point would be the abuse suffered by the Social Security system.

PERMIT

My occupational duties also included the management of the city's mobile home programs and overseeing the mobile home parks. This was a complicated process that encompassed rent control oversight and the issuance of operational permits. Kevin approached me and stated that he was handing over the management of the mobile home program to another employee named David. I was somewhat perplexed by this; David was a nice guy and a longtime employee, but he knew very little about state mobile home laws.

My assumption was that the city attorney was somehow behind this move. I didn't feel it was right to watch David fail, so I offered him my assistance. David refused my help, which I found odd as it was not like him. Though he should have accepted my offer, his inexperience led him to make a huge mistake. He conducted several hundred mobile home inspections, without providing the state-required occupation documents. This left the owners without the permits they paid for, which were required to legally occupy their residence. I advised David and Kevin of this misstep, but I was ignored. To this day I don't believe those residents have been provided with permits.

David's reasoning for refusing my help slowly started to unravel. Through his side occupation as a local preacher, David had close contacts with city council members. One such contact was a council member and fellow preacher who was the proponent for the hiring of Barbara. The council member also knew my complaint was the reason for Barbara leaving. He had apparently informed David and Kevin of his intention to make David my replacement. This was all I needed. Not only was the city attorney out to get me, but now I had a council member wanting me gone too.

These were not my only worries; at the time, the city was very concerned about racial diversity. They had been sued over discriminatory practices, aimed at low-income housing program participants. After losing the lawsuit, the city was mandated to conduct racially diverse public outreach programs and hiring techniques. The council member, Barbara, and David were all connected, and we did not share the same ethnicity. Because of the lawsuit, management was required to show they were promoting racial diversity.

Therefore, under the circumstances in the eyes of management, I presented the easiest option to dismiss.

Previously unknown to the public, the discrimination lawsuit which placed the mandates on the city had developed from the desires of the mayor. The mayor had often publicly voiced his opinion of reducing low-income housing participants and used Joe to help him with this goal. Before working for the city, the director, Joe, had previously held a county position. His role in the county was to oversee the low-income programs. While working for the county, Joe provided a list to Pamela of the local subsidized participants. I believe this was a request from the mayor and may have been part of the reason why Joe was given his job in the city.

Pamela created a rental inspection program, enabling her to target the local participants. She then divided up the list Joe provided and distributed it to her employees. We were instructed, by her, to inspect the participant properties in search of code violations. This was so Joe could have a reason to remove them from the program. At the time, I knew that this was unethical, and probably illegal, so I refused to comply with Pamela's order. I was not concerned about the repercussions from my noncompliance. I knew Pamela was smart enough not to place herself in a bad position. She was aware that if I had complained about the abuse of the list, she would have to deny allegations of her involvement.

COVID-19

My temporary stay of execution may have been granted, thanks only to the timing of the COVID-19 pandemic. The pandemic hit and the city immediately changed the way they conducted business, diverting their attention. Emergency operations were implemented: wearing masks, taking temperatures, and maintaining six-foot perimeters were now required. Each employee was provided with a six-foot long wooden dowel, to help gauge their distance from coworkers. This was implemented by the mayor as a control device to prevent any physical contact. At one point, the mayor even went so far as to say that if you did not get vaccinated, you would not have a job.

City programs and projects came to a halt, not a lot of actual work was being accomplished during this time. Many administrative personnel began to work from home, though I am still not convinced they were working at all. From the video conferences I was a part of, it appeared that they were just collecting a government paycheck to stay home and watch their kids. Of course, being rejected by and separated from the pack, I was not allowed this benefit. For me, the worst part of the pandemic was hearing the stories of the elderly who were passing away, while being kept from saying goodbye to their loved ones.

An emergency operations center was developed at city hall and activated during the pandemic. Assigned employees were required to work there on a rotating basis. The work mostly involved a bunch of overpaid government employees, pushing fake papers around and trying to appear busy. The real purpose of the center was to meet federally set guidelines that allowed access to more emergency funds. Public funds were constantly being syphoned from one government agency to another. The use of funds was dictated by the council. Because of this, programs were developed with the specific intent of bolstering the image of the elected officials.

To help distribute the newly acquired COVID funds, the council decided to create and donate gift cards to the citizens. The idea was for the cards to be used by the public to purchase meals from local restaurants. Since the funds for the cards originated from city public taxes, they were only to be used to benefit local businesses. Therefore, participating restaurants were required to be located within the incorporated area of the city. This plan sounded perfect, as everyone wanted a free meal, and it made the city officials look generous.

Officials instructed employees to quickly draft a plan, which was adopted by the council. Just under a million dollars of federal COVID funds would be used to sponsor the program. Individual cards would be worth twenty dollars each, just enough for a meal. The cards were to be distributed to citizens by city employees, starting with the council members and local bureaucrats. After they were used, the local restaurants would return the cards to the city for reimbursement.

A new employee by the name of Olivia was assigned to oversee the program. She was young, outgoing, and had physically attractive characteristics that she liked to flaunt, using provocative outfits. She had quickly become very close with the city manager. My office was just outside of hers, and I would overhear Olivia and Peter sitting for hours at work, discussing the latest television shows. It was well known in the city that you would advance quickly if you were assigned to a popular council backed project. Peter made it apparent by his response to her physical attributes, that she would too.

Olivia had been provided with an assistant to help her with the program. I would often have work-related dialogue with her assistant. During one such conversation she advised me that several different renditions of the card were developed before the mayor finally approved one. He would only accept and review the ones that had his picture prominently displayed on the front. She said that due to all the changes, the design cost for the first card alone was well above that of a new car. At least that of an economy car anyway, certainly not a car the mayor would be caught driving.

The cards were distributed like candy on Halloween, first to the council and then to the citizens. Through local gossip I learned that a couple of high-end restaurants, outside of the city limits, were also accepting the cards. Out of curiosity, I had my girlfriend Diane order from one of these restaurants to see if they would accept her gift card, and sure enough, they did. Since the restaurant was not located in the incorporated area, the city's economy would not benefit from the cards being used there. Regardless of its location, the restaurant owners were allowed to return the collected program cards for reimbursement. This did not surprise me, as the restaurant was owned by an ex-city official and his family. The prominent family members owned a lot of property in the city and had close contacts with current council members.

Accepting these redeemed cards meant the city was improperly dispensing hundreds of thousands of dollars, in public funds, to these restaurants. Since the cards were publicly known, the city could possibly be held liable for misuse of funds. Olivia was part of the department I worked for, so I felt it was my responsibility to say something. I notified Kevin and Olivia that there could be an issue. In response I was told by Kevin that this was already known, and that the restaurant would be reimbursed for the cards.

Arriving home that night, I felt sick to my stomach. I knew my only other option was to turn this over to the state. Supplying this information to the state would essentially mean that I was accusing the city of misappropriation of public funds. Since I had made Kevin aware of my knowledge, he would now know any details provided to the state would have come from me. Considering that I was already in the attorney's crosshairs, taking this step would surely mean the end of my career. From my understanding to this day, the city is still being allowed to operate programs in this manner.

CHAPTER EIGHT

Ages 50 and Up

The disheartening outcome of my discussion with Kevin, about the misuse of COVID funds, revealed to me my need to take another break from work. With the help of an internet social site, I was able to locate my old friend Ted. I contacted him and found out that he now had two grown children and was living in Southern California. Since he was close, only a couple of hours away, we set up a time we could meet.

Diane accompanied me on the drive down to unite with him. She enjoyed getting to meet my childhood friend and seeing me finally happy, being away from the issues at my job. In my conversations with Ted, I discovered that he had also joined the Army. He told me that his occupational specialty in the Army was that of a helicopter pilot. The same Ted who didn't want to fly in his grandfather's airplane was now a pilot. I thought what a small world it was, we both ended up in California after joining the Army to work on helicopters. Unfortunately, he informed me that his father and grandfather had passed years before, as had mine. Regardless, after thirty years gone by, it was nice to visit with my childhood friend.

Diane knew of a hotel and casino near Ted's house, where she wanted to stay. The hotel was surrounded by mountains that were filled with wildflowers, which made for a very romantic setting. This was the perfect place for us, and it was my chance to show her how much I cared for her. My unintentional emotional withdrawal, due to the stress from my job, had also taken a toll on Diane and my family. Though she continued to be patient with me, through some of these more difficult times, and I had been searching for the right opportunity to return her gesture. I had purchased a ring months before and locked it in the glove box of my truck. I guess I was waiting for the right time to bring it out of hibernation.

It was a beautiful warm summer day, so after we checked in, I asked if she would like to go for a walk down to a nearby pond. We ventured outside and were walking hand in hand, discussing some of the concerts we had attended together. I saw a small bench along the path we were walking, it had two rose bushes on either side that were in bloom and full of pink flowers. With this tranquil setting I thought, what better opportunity? I asked her to sit as I knelt before her and pulled the ring box from my pocket. Before I could open the box, she said the word "yes." I wasn't surprised she said yes, but I was a bit stunned at how quickly she did. I looked at her and said, "At least let me ask first." She replied, "No need." It was a very nice trip and just what I needed to take my mind off the city.

BRIBE

Upon returning to work, I found that more promotions and employee adjustments had taken place. Kevin advised me that both David and Olivia were being given promotions to manager positions. He told me that I would now be working under David. These promotions amounted to an increase of two classifications for both. Neither of them had reached even a supervisory level before the promotions, and as with others they were not required to submit applications. The promotions were handed out as a bonus would be, and as before other more qualified employees were not allowed to apply.

The two promotions reeked of political influence. Upset by this, I was once again left with my only recourse to make yet another complaint to HR, which I mistakenly made. I knew that the complaint wouldn't go far, but I still had to issue it. I felt at that point I had nothing left to lose; I was now sure they were after my job. I guess I was holding out hope that they would possibly change their minds. I was also thinking it would somehow make me feel better, but instead, it just added to my anxiety and made things worse.

It was a normal Thursday afternoon; I was in my office creating a spreadsheet on my city computer when I received a call from HR. I was asked by the manager to come up for a conversation. While walking through my department I noticed an uncommon silence and saw that there was no one at their desks. I began to contemplate what she might want to ask; I even started to trick myself into thinking maybe they were going to offer me a promotion. Though after seeing the empty department, I knew it may not be good, and they could possibly be escorting me to the gallows.

Upon my arrival to the second floor, I was brought to a small office area. In the office were my department director, whom I had never met but now worked for, the human resources manager, and the city manager. I was asked to sit down in a chair at the table, facing these three overpaid government employees. The city manager then handed me a letter with the words "NOTICE OF LAYOFF" at the top. I suddenly felt my body go numb; To them I was nothing more than a piece of rotten fruit, they had just released from their claws. I had fell from the city tree and onto a railway track below. Sitting on the track, I didn't know which way the train was coming from, but I knew I was about to get hit.

All I could now see before me were three large gray squirrels with their mouths full of nuts. They were staring down at me from the tree above, just waiting for me to react. I had nothing to say, but the same could not be said for Peter. Just as the words "sorry, but" began to leave his lips, I could feel the train strike me. Ran over by a train conducted by this arrogant gray squirrel, I was left on the track as flat as an envelope.

Their stairs inspired the feeling of worthlessness to saturate my soul. They did not see me as a person, rather just as an object, like the fruit that they just left flat as an envelope on the railway track. I felt like the envelope would, had it been placed in a mailbox with a stamp but no address, I now had no direction. As I had expected, the price I would pay for being released from their tyranny would be expensive, as the saying goes, freedom is never free.

Exiting the room with my head lowered in defeat, I felt deflated and demoralized. My embarrassment was only compounded by the presence of Joe. One of his final duties before he retired was to escort me from the building. During the slow painful journey, I did my best to maintain my composure, recalling the words of my late sergeant to never look down and question my heart. Though the trek was not made any easier by Joe's pathetic attempt at an empathetic speech, which was completely devoid of tact.

His caring nature, I could have only described as being derived from anal cancer, that had metastasized in his brain. Joe could have easily saved my job had he wanted to. He had just promoted his married secretary to a supervisory position, with whom he was having an affair. This is a position he could have provided to me, as she of course was not qualified for it, and it happened to be equal to mine at the time.

She was not the first of his personnel to be promoted that bowed to his lustful libido, he started doing this only to help avoid harassment lawsuits. This is something he learned from the city, after they used promotions to appease two of the employee complainants from the previous harassment lawsuits against him. These two employees were also given supervisory positions that I was more qualified for. As we walked, I was holding my newly acquired layoff documents in my right hand. Seeing his grin, I found myself wishing that I was ambidextrous, so that I could supply him with an attitude modifying smack with my left. Although, I would have had to borrow the violent nature of my ex-wife, as my morality would have prevented me from assaulting him.

After being laid off, I was forced to apply for early retirement, which I could not afford; these three squirrels stated the reason for my layoff, was their ability to hire an outside consultant to do my job. This was, of course, a lie; I had spoken to the consultants they wanted to use, so I knew that was not possible. After fifteen years, I had gained more institutional knowledge than they could replace using a consultant. The truth was that by making complaints about their inappropriate actions, I had become a liability to them.

Included with the termination notice was a document that they requested for me to review and sign. Reading the document, I saw that it was a hush money agreement; they were offering to pay me tens of thousands of dollars if I agreed not to talk. They gave me a week to consider, but after a few days deliberating, my consciousness got the best of me. I decided to decline their bribe money. After all, the money they offered would come from public funds, and it didn't come close to what they had just stolen from me. At fifty-one years old, I had only four years left to receive a full pension and lifetime medical insurance. They had taken all my benefits and half my pension, a loss I would not be able to recover from. With the click of his pen, Peter had stolen it all away.

SELLING

Since I did not take the city's bribe, I turned the wrongful termination complaint over to the state for investigation. It was time to let someone else deal with them, and who better than another government agency? Knowing how governments function, however, I had little confidence the city would ever be held responsible for their actions. But still, I was as interested in keeping them from hurting others, as I was in getting redemption. Intellectually I saw them as children, who kept taking candy from the dish on the table, that was meant for guests. If their actions were not corrected, they would continue to raid the candy bowl.

The pension I earned would simply not be enough to sustain me for my remaining years. Because of this, I searched my soul for weeks, trying to figure out what I was going to do next. Realizing I could retain my previous pension amount, if I obtained a similar job with another city in the state, I started to submit applications everywhere. I thought I still had some time left before the marketplace began to discriminate against my age. But it was quickly revealed to me that it was not my age, but my lack of a degree, that would hinder my employment. At one point I even applied to the city I had been working in when I was shot. Apparently, they had a short-term memory when it came to my personal sacrifice for them.

Without a job, I knew I could no longer afford my mortgage. The property I had purchased new, into which I had put thousands of hours of work, would have to go. I contacted a local real-estate agent I knew and asked him to list my house. Upon hearing of my recent layoff, Diane decided we should postpone the marriage. She advised me that she wanted to move back to her hometown in Texas. Since I had to sell anyway, this now made sense for both of us, as my son was there, and my mom was just in the next state. Diane then hired a company to move her personal property and flew to Texas to find a home for us to rent.

The process of cleaning out my belongings, and getting the house ready for the market, was mentally and physically exhausting for me; I had a lot of memories in this home. The move would also mean leaving my brothers and my friends. While packing my things, I discovered my half of the one dollar bill I had split with Tawnya over thirty years before. Thanks again to social networks, I located and contacted her. I told her about the half dollar I had found and to my amazement, she also still had hers.

In talking with her, I learned that she had married that boy from the Dear John letter she had given to me years before. She stated that they had a child together and were divorced soon after. Apparently, her father was the one that originally introduced them. She also divulged to me, that her father had been sentenced to twenty years in prison, for trafficking drugs. This information made his odd behavior years before more discernible. It also made me wonder, if it had been her that I had rescued from Chad, that day he attacked her, or really Chad whom I rescued, from her father's wrath.

OFFER

For me to move forward, it was necessary to leave my old life, and my Oregon childhood girlfriend behind. I continued to submit applications for government jobs, though it was now in Texas. While waiting for my home to sell, I received a call back from a city in Dallas, about an application I had submitted. They were interested in hiring me, and we set up an interview. The interview went well, and I was given a hire date. In the meantime, I was also contacted by the listing agent for my home, who had a buyer with an offer. The offer was below its current value, though I was told by my agent that it was the only offer I had received, and I should take it. After accepting the offer, I found out that my agent was less than honest with me.

The agent I had hired, I met while working for the city. He had held city real property disposition contracts. Hiring him was my mistake; I failed to perform my due diligence. For me growing older did not necessarily mean becoming wiser. When hiring him I wasn't considering the leverage the city might have on him. I was informed that he may have been pressured by the city to help get me out of town, before I changed my mind about selling. My theory was they were upset, because I did not except their bribe, and they were promising him future listings. I had seen how unscrupulous most real-estate agents were when it came to gathering more listings, so if this were true it wouldn't surprise me.

With my background in property sales, I knew that I didn't need an agent to buy or sell a home, and I should have sold mine "by owner." From my experience in selling a home, without multiple offers there seems to be no real advantage in using an agent. This is mainly because most of the transfer documents required for the transaction are completed by escrow agencies. It often seems that in a single offer situation, much of what a seller gains by having an agent can be lost by paying commissions. This, at least, is what I found as an individual homeowner. Of course, if you are an investor, pulling housing stock away from home buyers for profit, it's different. In that case, a knowledgeable agent could be beneficial by finding deals.

Though I blamed myself, I still decided to contact the state's real estate regulatory department about the occurrence. Unfortunately, they declined to investigate my complaint as I lacked significant evidence. Unlike my case with the city, all I had was rumors and statements. The department I contacted is funded by the fees collected from agents. Therefore, it makes sense why they would not want to have a claim against their own income source. This experience brought me to the conclusion that following my dream for this career, may not have resulted in success for me.

Years of working in property disposition demonstrated to me the lack of protection for homeowners' rights against investors, politicians, associations, and self-absorbed real-estate agents. Individual home buyers deal with competition from investors and the constant threat of ravenous fraud. After purchase, they endure homeowner authorities and local politicians who create laws to control the use of their property. Then upon selling, they are required to sign away their property rights and part of their equity to a broker, in a skewed sales contract. These one-sided contracts, while making brokers rich, can only ensure damage to the future of the industry. Though it is always the bad actions of the few that take advantage of others and cause more restrictions. As my mother would say, "Parasites should be removed before infections spread."

The issues with greed and deceit surrounding this profession are limited and were not created overnight by any one individual. Also, I am not one to take food from people's mouths, as I know agents must deal with a lot of competition when it comes to homeowners' equity. Homeowners are constantly fending off increasing utility costs, repair costs, and harassing venders. They also must deal with the constant bombardment of increasing exorbitant fees and taxes, instated by unrestrained local politicians. All of this can limit the equity a homeowner is left with to pay agents' commissions. Personally, I have nothing against professional real-estate agents. I only warn that even when entering this field with good intentions, it is easy to get caught up in seeing dollars and end up hurting the people you signed up to help.

To once again step off my soap box and make a long story short, I sold the home and moved to Texas. The job I was offered did not turn out to be as advertised. At my reception I was treated like an outsider and given the worst assignment location possible. To the other employees, I was seen as a guy from out of state taking up space at a local government job. After realizing this, I decided the job was not for me. I could not mentally handle going back to being just a nut amongst another bunch of squirrels. Upon my exit, the supervisor informed me that I would have a tough time finding employment around here, as I was older and an outsider. I found his comment disturbing, but at least it affirmed that I was making the right decision by not accepting the job.

PLAN

As it turned out he was right: starting a new career here would prove to be difficult. I submitted applications to several more cities in the area and attended a couple of interviews. This made me realize that I was indeed seen by them as an outsider. Once they found out I was from California, they all acted as if I was after their job. I thought this was what it must feel like to be an immigrant with an accent, legally in a country and trying to find employment. Without my friends and being viewed as a virus by the locals, I felt very alone and abandoned.

Assisting Diane in setting up our new rental home, helped to calm my mind and kept me from dwelling on my situation. I began to take a closer look at my financial options. Because I was let go just four years shy of receiving my lifetime medical coverage, I needed to find health insurance to purchase. While searching I found there were not many options, and it was very expensive. If I did not find work, the profit from the sale of my home would quickly be exhausted, just paying for my insurance. While reviewing my financial situation, I also saw that the survivor's benefit on my remaining pension would run out within ten years. This meant that within ten years, I would have nothing left to leave for my son. I didn't want to just waste away, exhausting my funds and not being able to find work.

While expanding my job search, I decided I needed some inspiration, and who better to get it from than Mom? She was only a four-hour drive away, so I jumped in my car and headed out. It was a great feeling knowing I could just pop in and surprise her. I encountered a few car accidents on the route to her home, so it took longer than I thought it would. By the time I arrived it was late in the day, and my mom was not home, though she had left the back door open for me. She was probably attending the day's last church service. I let myself in and made myself comfortable in a chair on her back porch.

Tired from the long drive, I closed my eyes to rest for a few minutes before my mom returned.

No sooner did I close my eyes, than the idea came to me, about how to resolve all my issues. I now knew what I had to do, and I started to set things in motion. I booked a ticket to California and spent the remainder of the day with my mother. She had always been there for me, and I couldn't go without letting her know how much I appreciated her. With my mom, no matter how hard I tried to keep my thoughts from her, she could always see right through me. It was mother's intuition. Regardless, I did the best I could to hide my sadness, as she had always done for me.

We went to dinner at a small local restaurant and talked about old times while we ate. She had built a huge porch at the back of her home where we spent the rest of the evening, just reminiscing. At one point she saw some squirrels just outside her window and commented to me, "Look, its squirrels collecting nuts, you better hide!" I just laughed while thinking, *It's a little late for that.*

At the end of my visit, my seventy-five-year-old mother drove me to the airport. This time, though, Dallas was just a stopover on my way to Los Angeles. My destination would be my old stomping grounds in the high desert. Driving down the freeway, my mother began looking for the airport exit. As she did, I thought, *I was also looking for an exit, but mine was to be far from all the squirrels that inhabited this place.* After saying goodbye to my mother, I put on a straight face and boarded the plane full of strangers. The flight was a disaster; it was crowded and bumpy. All the planes' passengers had blank stares on their faces. I found the abnormal cabin silence quite bizarre; no one talked the whole flight.

DOOR

Upon my arrival in Los Angeles, I took a taxi from the airport to my older brother's house. My brother is not a godly man like my mother, but he is very kind and always helped me when I needed him. He was surprised to see me, I explained to him that I was only in town for a few days. I told him that I would be going to the shooting range and would need to borrow my father's old handgun. My brother was of course happy to oblige my request.

After having a last meal with my brother, I set my alarm for 2:00 a.m., lay down on his couch, and tried to close my eyes. I knew there would be no sleep for me, but I had to keep up the show. The alarm went off, and I gathered my things and headed for the door. On my long walk, with all life's memories and emotions rushing through me, I wanted to cry but could only smile. Most of my thoughts were of my son and younger brother. My younger brother was now forty-six years old and had a family of his own, although in my mind, he was still my little brother. He overcame some hard times in his life and evolved into a successful businessman.

He was the most adventurous of us three, which is probably why he had more difficulties in life. His motto was, What type of life is more satisfying, an adventurous one or a boring one? This ideology, although fun, did come with consequences for him. Riding motorcycles, snow skiing, and water skiing, we took a lot of fun trips together and made some good memories. On one such trip, I accompanied him to Lake Havasu in Arizona for spring break. He had purchased a boat to enjoy on the lake and borrowed my father's small motor home for us to stay in. At the end of our weekend, we returned home with the motor home and the trailer and no boat. My brother's boat found a new permanent home at the bottom of the lake and did not make it home with us.

The thoughts of my brother were disrupted by my arrival at my destination, where I sat down to rest after my long walk. So many thoughts had run through my mind that my head felt like a sieve separating them all. Trying to relax my thoughts, I leaned my head back against the steel metal door. The cold, hard steel pressing against the back of my head, felt like a synopsis for my adult life. I was sitting in front of the rear entry door to City Hall, across from Peter's parking spot. I didn't want to sit and think too long, or I would not be able to go through with it. I placed the barrel of the gun in my mouth, as I knew this would be the most effective method.

"Click" was the next sound I heard; the misfire stunned me. Despite my confused state, I realized that if it had discharged and I was still alive, I would have been left with the distinct taste of gunpowder residue. Instead of being relieved, I became agitated; my plan had succumbed to failure. I had set this up perfectly; it had taken all my emotional strength just to get to this point. Although very frustrating, the sound was also a relief. I pulled the gun barrel from my mouth and examined the gun. The single hollow-point bullet, I had carefully placed in the chamber, was still lined up with the barrel. It was a misfire. I took the bullet out and examined it. The primer was intact, and there was nothing wrong with the bullet.

As I pressed my tongue to the roof of my mouth to see if I could taste the powder residue, I could hear my mom's voice saying, "We plan, God laughs." I knew then that my thought process was wrong. I was thinking with my mind and not my heart. Suddenly I again heard my mother's voice saying, "Get up before they see you." Her words caused me to open my eyes, and standing before me was my mother. Looking around, I realized that I was still sitting on the chair on her porch, and she was apparently talking to my aunt on the phone. I must have fallen asleep while waiting for her. It had all been a bad dream, and she was trying to wake me up before my aunt arrived.

In a complete daze, and too embarrassed to tell my mother of my dream, I pulled my phone from my pocket and called Diane. I told her what had happened, and she replied, "Get yourself up and get back here. You have another job offer." Since I was left with no better plan, I followed her instructions. On the drive back, Diane and I talked about why things had come to this for me. She asked me, "Is there anything that helps you not to think about the bad things in your life?" I thought as hard as I could and replied, "When I was writing documents at work, the only thing I was able to concentrate on were the words on the page." She said, "Then write words on a page!"

BOOK

Since my bad dream had not yet become reality, I felt I had been given a chance to change my story's outcome, so I set about writing as Diane suggested I should. At first it was frustrating, attempting to avoid all the emotional triggers, and I considered having someone to help me write it. Then I started to think about the city newsletters from the mayor, that were written by his secretaries and only signed by him. I needed this to be from my perspective; I didn't want to sign a document made by someone else. We all need to tell our own stories in our own way, we lived them, and they belong to us.

Many modern songs and stories, published for public entertainment, seem to celebrate evil. Instead of celebrating it, I preferred my writing to expose it. I wanted to take inspiration from those who had shown me the benefits of honesty and of helping others. I needed to demonstrate that this can create a better existence than the celebration of materialistic possessions. To accomplish this, I started with my fondest childhood memories. This brought me to my parents and the wisdom they shared with me in my tutoring. From them I did not inherit financial wealth, but what I did inherit I cherish much more. My father taught me how to appreciate nature in all its forms. Because of him I could build my own car or my own house. My mother taught me how to build a life and a family.

It was also important for me to reveal the trials and tribulations in my work life, and my encounters with the triumphant human spirit. After I completed the book, Diane was the first one to read it, and she said, "Well, you have finally found it."

I replied, "Found what?"

She looked at me and said, "You found your gift. Everyone is given a gift in life, and it is up to us to find it."

Her statement made me realize that I still had a reason to live and something to share that could help others.

While writing the book, I accepted the job that was offered to me, during my last visit with my mom. The position was ideal, it was in a city only a few miles from where Diane and I now lived. The kindness of my new coworkers erased my feelings of insecurity about fitting in here. Although the pay was less than half of my previous salary and there was no real sustainable pension, the job duties were more than fulfilling. I was received with open arms, and I found no squirrel traps. The employees were allowed to communicate freely with each other. Their speech, like mine, was filled with harmless sarcasm, only theirs was improved with southern charm.

There is still a state investigator assigned to my claim. However, the state might not be a reliable source for transparency and protection. Therefore, this book may be the only way my story could be told. Still filled with doubt, I try to remain hopeful that the investigators will help to correct these purposefully perpetrated government mistakes. Though I equate bringing the state the case to that of starting a complaint with the city human resources department. Most employees don't realize that although these departments may act friendly, they are not your friends. Their objection is to represent and protect the entity they work for, and moreover to preserve their own self-image.

Tinnitus and PTSD continue to plague me, although I deal with these by losing myself in my writing. Regardless of my feelings, I try always to place importance on maintaining honesty and open communication with others. My goal remains the prioritization of respecting our rights to the freedom of speech that our soldiers fought for. I know that by telling my story, I may be putting myself in danger. But for me, if there was a reason to set aside my need for security and take the chance of being buried like a nut in the hands of greedy squirrels, this would be it. Telling the story keeps the memory alive and like with betrayal, it is more difficult to destroy evidence of misconduct, when it exists as a memory.

Living a life of servitude and repaying those who have helped me has brought me joy, and therefore is something I will continue to do. In this process, I will always refuse to sacrifice my morals and standards to appease others. I believe that if we are to live a life of service, then we need to live it for those who deserve it. My story does not end here; it is still being written. This is just the end of my book. Thanks to those who believe in me and love me, my story will continue.

It is time now for you to put down this book and finish writing yours. My hope is for you to live a full life and learn something from your every adventure, as I have in mine. Try to allow the memories of lessons gained through adventures, to guide you and serve as a reminder to help in determining your future actions. This model has allowed me to intercept bad decisions, preventing me from making mistakes, allowing me to avoid negative experiences, and providing me with more positive memories.

Thank you for joining me and allowing me to share my journey with you. We are all destined to leave this place someday, so there is no need to rush things. If you ever find yourself at the end of your rope, try to remember, as Diane told me, we all have a gift to share. Instead of squirreling your gift away, consider sharing it before you go. Sharing your gift may not only provide others with inspiration, but in the end like with me, it just might be your own savior.

Epilogue

fter years of working for the government, if I had to sum it up in one word, it would be "estranged." Once a person becomes trapped in a politically charged environment, they tend to pull away from reality and become estranged to the struggles of others.

Climbing the ladder of success in government often requires you to replace your beliefs with the priorities of your mentors, whose egos have long since caused their own beliefs to become corrupt.

This corruption takes place slowly over time. The more they are praised for their actions, the more powerful they feel. As their ego grows, they begin to feel invincible, ignoring the reality of the world around them. At some point, they will stop listening to the citizens they were meant to serve.

In life, from what I have seen, this scenario of creating engorged egos is not limited to government. Corporations and celebrities have also been caught up in this struggle for money and power.

Of course, I am aware that there are much larger issues at hand when it comes to human rights and the world. But as my father would tell me while I was looking at the rusted old GTO project, "You have to start somewhere, kiddo."

I will always believe that true happiness comes from providing kindness and generosity to strangers. If you take one thing from my book, please let it be this: No matter where you are in life, try not to become estranged to the struggles of others, after all where would you be without them.

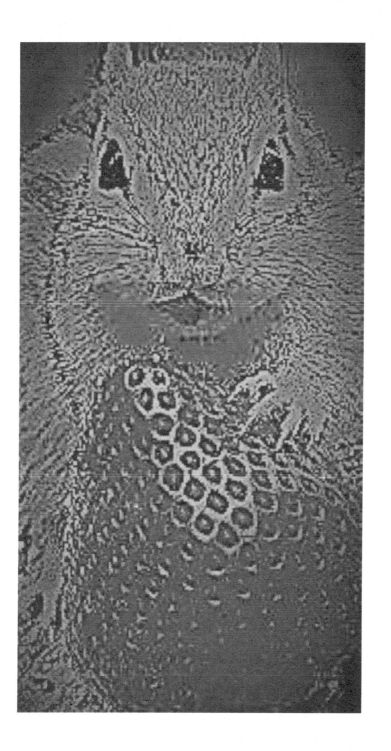